Women Who Rock the Stage

Captivate and Impact Any Audience Virtually, Face to Face or Anywhere You Show Up

Author of Unstoppable Woman

Founder of The Women's Empowerment Society

Marsha Lynn Hudson, EdS

"The Queen of Systems"

ISBN -979-8-218-79385-2

First Edition: 2025

Published by Marsha Hudson Media

Why I Wrote This Book

I wrote *Women Who Rock the Stage* because I know what it feels like to have something to say—but not always know how to say it with power, clarity, and confidence.

As a college professor, I've spent years standing in front of classrooms. I've spoken at conferences, led workshops, and written books. But let me be honest—it didn't come naturally. I had to learn how to step into my presence, silence my doubts, and show up in a way that connected with others. But you don't have to be a professor, keynote speaker, or seasoned workshop host to rock the stage.

Maybe you just know, deep down, that your story matters. That your voice carries wisdom. That your message could transform someone's life if you just had the tools and courage to share it.

That's who I wrote this book for.

For the woman who's ready to speak up—not just on a stage, but in a room, on a Zoom, in a training, in a conversation, or online.
For the woman who has lived through some things, learned from her journey, and now wants to lead, coach, teach, and empower others with her words.
For the woman who's tired of shrinking, hiding, or second-guessing—and is finally ready to walk boldly in her purpose.

You were never meant to stay silent.
You were born to stand up, speak up, and show up fully as who you are.
Let this book be your guide.

This Book Is for You If...

 You have a story, a message, or a mission—and you're ready to share it with the world.
You want to grow your confidence, own your voice, and speak with purpose.
 You dream of leading workshops, hosting events, landing speaking gigs, or just showing up more boldly in the spaces you're in.
You've struggled with fear, self-doubt, or wondering if your voice really matters.
You're ready to take your platform—big or small—and use it for impact, income, and influence.

If that sounds like you, then *welcome*. This book was written with you in mind. You're not just meant to speak— you're meant to shift rooms.

How to Use This Book- It is a Blueprint and a Guide- You need a pen in hand!

This isn't a book to read and shelf. It's a tool. A playbook. A guide to help you rock every stage you step on—whether it's a mic in your hand, a camera in your face, or a boardroom full of decision-makers.

Here's how to get the most out of it:

Read one chapter at a time. Each one builds your mindset, skillset, and strategy. No fluff—just what you need to grow.

Reflect as you go. Jot down your thoughts, underline powerful lines, and think about how each lesson applies to your own journey.

Practice. Show up. Apply it. Whether it's going live on social media, pitching a speaking gig, or speaking up in a meeting—this book is meant to push you to take bold action.

Pair it with the companion journal. I created a journal that goes hand-in-hand with this book to help you dive deeper, map out your vision, and track your growth as a speaker and leader.

You're here because you're ready. Flip the page, grab your highlighter, and let's start your next chapter because **you are a woman who rocks the stage**- virtually, F2 F or anywhere you show up.

Marsha Lynn Hudson- The Queen of Systems
www.marshalynnhudson.com
Email- marsha@marshalynnhudson.com

- For the free audio training to accompany this book- go to: https://marshalynnhudson.podia.com/

Dedication and Acknowledgments

This book is dedicated to my husband, Malcolm Hudson who is my best friend and supporter. Thank you for all you do for me, and thank you for our life of joy and peace that we share together. I thank God for you daily. Thank you being a man of faith, and for helping me to be stronger in my faith.

I want to thank God for the life he has given me, for always taking care of me, and for always providing for me. He has never failed me or left me and he will do the same for you.

I want to dedicate this book to my wonderful praying sisters and brother- Pat, Linda, Renee, Loretha, Brenda and Zo. I want to thank my awesome family who are always in my corner, and all of you on the family text chat filling me with laughter, joy, love and prayer daily. You are all my people.

I also want to acknowledge my 2 prayer partners, Misty Allmond and Holly Canty for always counseling me in the word day in and out. To my good friends, great neighbors, colleagues, clients, women business associates, followers and supporters- you all know who you are.

Lastly, thank you to the SBDC directors, and all of the decision makers over the years who have allowed me to speak and train on your stages virtually and face to face.

To all of you-- I want you to know that you are all a part of my ...

"why."

If you're reading this and you've supported me in any way — as family, a friend, a client, or a colleague — please know I carry your kindness in these words and beyond.

Special Note

How to Turn Conversations Into Cash

Every stage you step on, every podcast you guest on, and every room you walk into is more than just a chance to speak — it's a chance to spark transformation and opportunity. The truth is, when you learn how to turn conversations into cash, you stop leaving money on the table and start using your influence to open new doors.

Speaking isn't just about sharing information; it's about building connection. When you share your story, your strategies, and your solutions, you aren't just talking — you're creating trust. And trust is the currency that turns an audience member into a client, a follower into a buyer, and a conversation into a contract.

Think about it: people don't buy products or services, they buy into *people*. They buy into stories, into voices they can relate to, into leaders who show up with authenticity. If you can stand on a stage, in a boardroom, on a Zoom call, or even at a coffee shop and clearly share your value, you can captivate not just hearts — but wallets.

Turning conversations into cash is not about being "salesy." It's about being strategic. It's about weaving your offers and your expertise naturally into your message so your audience sees the next step as obvious. When you speak with clarity, you guide people toward transformation. And transformation is always worth investing in.

The beauty is that you don't have to change who you are or learn a script. You simply learn how to position your message with intention. You learn how to share stories that highlight problems you solve, ask questions that open doors, and use simple frameworks that invite your audience to lean in and want more from you.

When you master this skill, every platform becomes profitable. Your keynote can lead to consulting contracts. Your breakout session can lead to book sales. Your panel discussion can lead to coaching clients. Even casual networking can turn into paid opportunities when you confidently own your message.

That's why this book isn't just about speaking; it's about monetizing your message. You have the power to inspire, the ability to lead, and the influence to impact lives. And when you learn to turn conversations into cash, you step into the next level — where your voice is not only heard, but valued.

The Step-by-Step Process to Turn Conversations Into Cash

Step 1: Create a Lead Magnet
The very first step is to give your audience something of value for free. This could be a guide, checklist, template, or mini training — something quick they can download that positions you as the expert and keeps you top of mind. Your lead magnet is the bridge between someone being inspired by you and wanting to stay connected with you.

Step 2: Nurture with Email
Once they download your lead magnet, don't leave them hanging. Begin nurturing the relationship with a welcome email that introduces who you are and how you help. Then send consistent follow-up emails that share tips, stories, and strategies. Email builds trust and keeps you in front of the people who've already raised their hand to learn from you.

Step 3: Build Consistency and Connection
Nurturing doesn't happen in one email — it happens over time. Continue to send emails that provide encouragement, education, and insight. Think of it as small touches that deepen the relationship. This is where you move from being a voice they've heard once to being the mentor or leader they trust.

Step 4: Extend an Invitation
When you've built rapport, invite your audience to a next step. That could be a free strategy session, a breakthrough call, or a discovery conversation. The call is where you go deeper, listen, ask the right questions, and uncover the problems they want solved.

Step 5: Present Your Offers
During the call, you aren't "selling" — you're serving.

Share how you can help and present your offers clearly. People appreciate being told exactly how they can work with you. This is where conversations turn into contracts, strategy turns into sales, and your voice becomes your vehicle for profit.

Bonus Pathways: Social Media & LinkedIn
Not every conversation happens on stage. Sometimes it starts with a post, a DM, or a comment. By consistently posting good content and offering value, you attract people who are ready for more. On platforms like LinkedIn, you can easily transition from a comment to a direct message, then to a call — and ultimately, into a paying client.

Table of Contents

Chapter 1

From Fear to Fearless – The Mindset of a

Powerful Speaker

"You don't have to be fearless to start — you just have to be willing."

Fear will always try to ride shotgun when you decide to do something bold with your life—especially when you decide to use your voice. Speaking on a stage, whether virtual or in person, comes with a level of vulnerability most people run from. It's not just the fear of forgetting your words— it's the fear of being seen, judged, misunderstood. That's real.

But here's what I want you to know: the women you admire most weren't fearless when they started—they were just willing to move forward anyway. Fear doesn't disappear before you step up—it loses power the moment you do. Your story, your voice, your perspective—they matter more than your nerves ever will.

I used to believe that powerful speakers were just born confident. That they walked on stage without an ounce of self-doubt. But that's not true. What makes a speaker powerful is not the absence of fear, but their ability to keep speaking in spite of it. The most magnetic speakers are the ones who feel the fear and still show up with heart and honesty. They're not trying to be perfect—they're trying to connect. You don't need flawless delivery. You need truth, courage, and a message you believe in. If your voice shakes, let it shake—and speak anyway.

Every woman has a message inside her. But for many of us, that message stays locked behind years of insecurity, comparison, and silence. Maybe you were told you were too loud. Or not loud enough. Maybe someone laughed at your idea, or you convinced yourself you didn't have what it takes. That ends here. Your voice wasn't given to you just to survive—it was given to you to serve. The people who need your message don't care about your grammar, your slide deck, or your outfit. They care about your heart. And they need to hear it.

The mindset of a powerful speaker starts with one truth: you are already enough. You don't need to wait until you lose the weight, get the degree, or land your first paid gig. Start where you are. With what you know. With what you've lived. Speaking is like a muscle. It builds with use, not just theory. And every single time you speak, you get closer to the woman you're becoming.

One of the most common fears is the fear of not being good enough. That fear whispers, "Who do you think you are?" But the better question is—who do you think you're here to serve? When you shift your mindset from me to mission, the fear begins to shrink. You're not just speaking to impress; you're speaking to impact. And when you focus on the people who need your words, the pressure to perform starts to fade. This is not about being the best speaker in the room—it's about being the most real.

You don't have to sound like anyone else to be powerful. You don't need to mimic someone else's delivery, energy, or voice. Your story, told in your voice, with your personality—that's what makes you magnetic. People remember authenticity more than polish. You can be professional and still be you. Let your quirks shine. Let your heart lead. The more you sound like yourself, the more people will lean in and trust you.

We all start somewhere. My first talk? I was nervous, my voice cracked, and I forgot half of what I wanted to say. But people came up to me afterward with tears in their eyes—not because I was perfect, but because I was honest. I spoke from a place of truth, and it reached them. That day taught me something I've never forgotten: people don't need perfection—they need connection. Your vulnerability will open more doors than your credentials ever could.

To become fearless, you have to start small. Say yes to the local panel. Volunteer to speak on Zoom. Go live on Instagram for five minutes. These "small" actions are really big wins in disguise. Each one chips away at fear's power. You'll start to build confidence one rep at a time. And one day, you'll look back and realize—you're no longer the woman who was scared to raise her hand. You're the woman with the mic, owning her truth and changing lives.

When you speak, speak from your power—not your perfection. Speak from your why. Think of the woman sitting in your audience who's just one decision away from changing her life. She doesn't need you to be flawless. She needs you to be bold enough to go first. Every time you speak up, you give someone else permission to rise. That's leadership. And that's what fearless speaking is really about. It's not ego. It's impact.

You're not just here to give a talk. You're here to deliver transformation. That shift in mindset—from "I'm just a speaker" to "I'm a vessel for change"—will elevate your entire presence. So stop shrinking to fit spaces you were meant to stretch. Stop waiting for the fear to go away before you begin. Speak, even when your voice trembles. Speak, even if only one person hears you. Because one person is enough. And you never know who's healing on the other side of your story.

Believing you belong in the space you want to occupy is the very first step toward owning your voice. Too often, women hold themselves back because they are waiting to feel "ready." But readiness doesn't show up before you start—it's something that develops as you take action. The more you speak, write, post, or share your message, the more you start to believe in your ability to do it. Confidence grows when you keep promises to yourself, even the small ones. If you say you're going to post on social media once a week, follow through. If you commit to sending that proposal, send it. Over time, these small, consistent actions create the belief that you are exactly where you're supposed to be.

Taking the first step is always the hardest, but momentum builds when you keep moving. Think about the times you've started something new—it might have felt awkward or uncomfortable at first, but with repetition, it became easier. That's how speaking, writing, and sharing your message works too. The more you do it, the more natural it feels. You'll learn what resonates with your audience and what doesn't. You'll find your rhythm, your tone, and your confidence. And before you know it, the thing that once terrified you becomes second nature.

It's important to remember that every successful person you admire once started at the beginning too. They didn't magically wake up confident and skilled—they grew into it by showing up over and over again. They failed, adjusted, and kept going. They didn't let one mistake convince them they weren't good enough. Instead, they used mistakes as lessons. This mindset shift changes everything, because you stop seeing challenges as proof you can't do it and start seeing them as proof you're learning. That's where real growth happens.

Your voice will get stronger as you use it. Just like a muscle, it develops with practice and effort. You don't need to have the perfect words right away. The more you share, the more you refine your message and learn how to connect with people in a deeper way. Your audience doesn't expect perfection—they expect you to show up. And every time you do, you're building a foundation of trust. Trust is what keeps people coming back to hear from you again and again.

The fear of not being good enough is one of the biggest barriers to starting. I've been there, wondering who would even want to hear from me, thinking my story didn't matter enough. But here's what I've learned—your story is exactly what makes you valuable. Nobody else has your exact perspective, your life lessons, or your voice. People connect to authenticity, not perfection. When you show up as yourself, flaws and all, you give others permission to do the same. Your courage becomes contagious. And that's what inspires people to lean in and listen.

At the end of the day, you have to decide that your voice matters enough to be heard. No one else can give you that permission—it has to come from you. You get to choose whether fear or faith leads your decisions. Fear will keep you silent, but faith will push you forward. And when you move forward, even if it's one small step at a time, you create opportunities you couldn't have imagined before. Your message is needed. Your story can change lives. And it all starts when you decide to speak.

Milestone Marker

By the end of this chapter, you should have:

- A clear one-sentence core message that defines what you stand for.
- The confidence to introduce yourself without fumbling or over-explaining.
- A starting point for building every talk, post, or offer around your core message.

Get Paid!

Here's the shift I want you to make early—you are not "just" sharing a message, you are delivering value that solves problems, inspires change, and motivates action. That has a price. Speaking is not just a passion—it can be a business, and a very profitable one.

Organizations, companies, conferences, and associations have budgets for speakers. They expect to pay for expertise. Your lived experience, insight, and strategies are expertise. The moment you start seeing yourself as a problem-solver and change-maker, the easier it becomes to ask for payment without hesitation.

To start getting paid, you need to position yourself as a professional. That means having a speaker bio, a polished headshot, and clear descriptions of your talk topics with specific outcomes. Know your rates and practice saying them with confidence. If you're just starting, you may offer reduced rates or barter for testimonials, professional photos, or video footage—but do it with a plan to move quickly into paid engagements. Being paid is not just about money—it's about respect for the time, energy, and preparation you put into your craft. You're not just giving a talk. You're creating an experience and delivering transformation. Own your value and others will too.

Problem & Solution

Problem: Most women never step into their voice because fear tells them they're not enough—too old, too late, too messy, too unknown.
Solution: You don't need to be perfect—you just need to be real. Fear fades when you step into your mission. Confidence comes from doing, not waiting.

Imagine this Scenario

She had been speaking on stages for years but always felt like something was missing. Her talks were good, but they lacked focus—no signature message, no clear direction. One day, she decided to dig deep and define what she truly wanted to be known for. She got clarity on her core message, gave it a name, and began delivering it with purpose. That shift changed everything.

The next time she spoke, the audience leaned in. People came up to her afterward saying, "I felt like you were talking to me." She started getting invitations to speak, not just because she was good—but because she was *clear*. Once she owned her message, she finally owned the room.

My Mindset Shift

I used to believe I needed a big audience to be taken seriously. I watched what others were doing and tried to copy their strategies—thinking I had to look a certain way, price my offers low, and constantly chase recognition. I thought if I wasn't a 6- or 7-figure speaker, no one would listen.

But that wasn't true. What I needed was my own voice, my own framework, and my own value. Once I stopped chasing numbers and focused on serving, everything changed. I built my business from the ground up—not by being flashy, but by being consistent and bold in my purpose. And now? My business is taking off on my own terms.

Words of Wisdom

I used to wait until I "felt ready" to speak—until I realized readiness is a decision, not a feeling. The most powerful shift I made was deciding to show up scared. And I never looked back.

Step-by-Step Action Plan: From Fear to Fearless

1. Write down the three fears you have about speaking.
2. Rewrite each one as an empowering belief.
3. Create a 30-second "why I speak" statement.
4. Practice speaking it out loud every day for 7 days.
5. Say yes to one small speaking opportunity this month (even if it's on Zoom or IG Live)

Quick Wins

- Write your speaker affirmation and post it where you can see it daily.
- Follow three women speakers who inspire you.
- Record a one-minute message to your future self as a speaker.
- Tell a friend, "I'm ready to use my voice."
- Join a speaker-focused Facebook group or virtual community.

Journal Prompt

What would change in your life, business, or confidence if you stopped letting fear silence you?

_____

_____

_____

Reflection

My biggest takeaway:

_____

My next move:

_____

Key Points to Remember

- Fear is normal, but it's not the boss.
- You don't need to be perfect—you just need to be real.
- Confidence is built by doing.
- Your story matters.
- Speak from power, not perfection.
- You never know who's waiting on the other side of your message.

Mic Drop Moment

"You were not given a voice to stay silent. You were given a voice to set people free."

Affirmation- Say It

"I have something powerful to say. I release fear and rise in purpose. I am a speaker with a message that matters."

Prompt for AI

Act as a speaking confidence coach. Write three daily affirmations and a short, simple morning ritual I can follow to overcome fear and step into my voice.

Smart Thinking: You don't need permission to be powerful. Start where you are, with what you know, and speak from that place of truth. When you own your message, you shift from doubting to leading.

Common Mistakes and How to Avoid Them

- **Mistake:** Trying to share too many ideas in one talk.
  Avoid it: Focus on one powerful takeaway that sticks.
- **Mistake:** Copying someone else's message or style.
  Avoid it: Your uniqueness is your power. Speak in your own voice.
- **Mistake:** Waiting until you feel "ready."
  Avoid it: Start sharing your message now— confidence comes through practice.

Step Into the Spotlight Recap

Owning your message is the first step in becoming a speaker who rocks the stage. When you are clear, people listen. When you're confident, people respond. Step into the spotlight knowing your message isn't just words—it's the foundation of your impact and your business.

Implementation Assignment

Write your **signature message in one sentence.** Practice saying it out loud three times today—once in the mirror, once to a friend, and once on video (even if you don't post it). Notice how it feels to *own* your message.

Speaker's Get Paid Checklist

1. Create a professional speaker bio (short and long versions).
2. Get a quality headshot that represents your personality and brand.
3. List your speaking topics with clear outcomes and benefits.
4. Prepare a one-page speaker sheet with your bio, topics, testimonials, and contact info.
5. Set your starting rates and create a tiered pricing structure.
6. Build a simple speaker page or section on your website.
7. Start collecting testimonials from every speaking engagement.
8. Record at least one professional-quality video of you speaking.

9. Build a contact list of potential organizations, events, and decision-makers.
10. Practice confidently stating your fee without hesitation.

Chapter 2

Own Your Message, Own the Room –

Building a Signature Message That Sticks

*"When you own your message, you own the room—
whether it's five people or five hundred."*

Every great speaker has one thing in common: a message so clear and so rooted in who they are that people can repeat it after they leave the room. That's the power of a signature message. It's not just about what you say—it's about what people remember, repeat, and act on after hearing you speak.

When I first started speaking, I tried to talk about *everything*. I wanted to inspire, teach, motivate, and encourage—all in one breath. But here's the truth: when you try to speak on everything, you dilute your impact. People don't walk away knowing what you stand for. Owning your message means deciding what you want to be known for—and building everything you say on that foundation.

A signature message is not a fancy slogan. It's the heartbeat of your speaking career. It's the one thing you want people to connect to your name. When someone hears your message, they should instantly think, "That's her. That's what she's about."

Breaking through life's challenges starts with acknowledging that you can't control everything, but you can control how you respond. Life will always bring situations that test your patience, strength, and faith. It's tempting to focus on what's not fair or what's too hard, but that mindset will keep you stuck. Instead, you have to shift your focus toward what you can do, even if it's one small step. Sometimes, that step is simply getting out of bed and choosing to try again. Other times, it's having the courage to make a big decision that scares you. Either way, every step you take is proof that you're still in the fight. And that's what matters—you're still moving forward.

The truth is, challenges aren't meant to break you; they're meant to shape you. They reveal strength you didn't know you had. When you look back at the struggles you've overcome, you'll notice that those moments grew your resilience the most. You learned how to keep going when it didn't seem possible. You figured out how to adapt when the plan fell apart. And you discovered that you're capable of more than you thought. Every single challenge has left you with tools, lessons, and courage you can use for the next one. That's how growth works—it's built in the hard seasons.

When you're facing something difficult, it's easy to think you're the only one who's ever been through it. But you're not alone, even when it feels like it. There are people who have walked a similar road and made it to the other side. Their stories are proof that you can make it too. This is why surrounding yourself with the right people is so important. You need voices that remind you of your strength when you forget it yourself. You need encouragement, truth, and sometimes even a push. Community can make the difference between quitting and persevering.

One of the biggest keys to overcoming challenges is refusing to let them define you. What you're going through is a chapter in your story, not the whole book. You might feel stuck right now, but this is temporary. You have the power to decide how the story unfolds from here. You can choose to learn from it, grow from it, and use it to help others later. You can decide that this is the moment you get stronger, wiser, and more determined. That choice is yours alone to make. And once you make it, everything changes.

You also have to give yourself permission to feel what you feel. Pretending you're fine when you're not doesn't help you heal—it just buries the pain deeper. It's okay to cry, to admit you're scared, or to acknowledge that you're tired. That doesn't make you weak; it makes you human. The strength comes in choosing to keep going even when those feelings are still there. You don't have to wait until you "feel" strong to move forward. Strength is built in the middle of the storm, not after it's over.

At some point, you have to believe that the challenge you're facing can be the very thing that elevates you. What if this struggle is preparing you for something bigger? What if it's teaching you the exact lessons you'll need for your next season? You may not see the purpose right now, but that doesn't mean it's not there. Keep showing up, keep doing the work, and keep your heart open to the possibility that something good can come from this. One day, you'll look back and realize this season was the turning point. And you'll be glad you didn't give up.

Milestone Marker

By the end of this chapter, you should have:

- Identified what makes your brand unique and memorable.
- Updated at least one place online (bio, profile, or website) to reflect your message.
- Chosen 1–2 platforms where you'll consistently show up to build visibility.

Why Owning Your Message Matters

When your message is unclear, three things happen:

1. People can't remember you.
2. They can't tell others about you.
3. They can't book you—because they don't know what you do.

But when your message is clear, everything changes. You become memorable. You stand out in a crowded market. And you make it easy for people to refer you, book you, and pay you.

The Trap of Copying Others

I've seen too many speakers try to mimic someone else's style, story, or delivery. They think, "If it worked for her, maybe it will work for me." But copying someone else only makes you sound like a second-rate version of them. Your power is in your originality. You've lived a life no one else has. You've overcome challenges no one else has faced in the exact same way. That's your gold. That's what will connect you to your audience.

5 Branding Mistakes That Keep You Invisible and Underpaid

Even the most passionate, talented women can stay stuck if their brand isn't working for them. These five mistakes are the most common traps I see—and the most costly. If you're not getting noticed, booked, or paid, you might be making one of them.

Mistake #1: Blending In Instead of Standing Out

What it looks like: Trying to copy what everyone else is doing online—same language, same look, same offers.
Why it hurts you: You become forgettable. And when people can't remember you, they can't choose you.
Reframe it: *"I don't need to be everywhere. I need to be clear, bold, and me."*
Smart Reflection: What makes your voice, story, or approach different? Lean into that.

Mistake #2: Leading with Your Title, Not Your Transformation

What it looks like: Saying "I'm a coach," "I'm a speaker," or "I help everyone."
Why it hurts you: Titles don't sell. Results do. People pay for transformation, not general information.
Reframe it: *"I don't just tell people what I do—I show them what they get."*
Smart Reflection: What specific result or outcome do you help people achieve?

Mistake #3: Inconsistent Online Presence

What it looks like: Posting randomly, showing up on five platforms for a week, then disappearing.

Why it hurts you: Trust and credibility are built with consistency. Silence creates doubt.

Reframe it: *"If I want to be known, I have to be seen— regularly."*

Smart Reflection: Where do you want to show up consistently for the next 30 days?

Mistake #4: No Clear Offer or Call to Action

What it looks like: Sharing great content but never telling people how to work with you.

Why it hurts you: Inspiration without invitation leaves money and impact on the table.

Reframe it: *"It's not pushy to invite—it's a service."*

Smart Reflection: What's one simple, clear way someone can take the next step with you?

Mistake #5: Building Without a Brand Message

What it looks like: Having a logo, colors, and website—but no clear message that connects.

Why it hurts you: People don't buy pretty—they buy clarity. If your message is muddy, your brand is forgettable.

Reframe it: *"My brand is built on my message, not my marketing."*

How to Find Your Signature Message

1. **Look at your story.** What themes keep showing up? Overcoming fear? Leadership? Transformation?
2. **Listen to your audience.** What do people thank you for? What do they say "hit home" after you speak?
3. **Ask yourself:** If someone could only remember one thing about me, what would I want it to be?

Implementation Assignment

Update your **bio or introduction** to reflect your personal brand. Keep it simple: Who you help, what transformation you bring, and why it matters. Post it on one platform today—or practice saying it the next time you introduce yourself.

The goal is not perfection—it's practice. The more you own it, the more natural it will feel when the spotlight is on you.

Get Paid!

Owning your message is not just about confidence—it's about positioning yourself for income. Event planners, companies, and organizations pay for *clarity*. They want to know exactly what they're getting when they hire you. The more specific and consistent your message is, the more valuable you become.

If you want to get paid to speak, you have to:

- Package your message into a clear topic with outcomes.

- Create a short and long version of your talk so you can adapt to any audience.
- Market that talk consistently so people know you as *the* person for that message.

Problem & Solution

Problem: Many speakers can't get booked or build momentum because their message is too broad or unclear.

Solution: Narrow your focus. Create a clear, repeatable message that aligns with your expertise and your passion.

Imagine this Scenario

For years, she shared valuable content, but no one seemed to notice. She was blending in, lost in the noise online. That all changed when she decided to build her personal brand with intention. She clarified her niche, updated her messaging, and started showing up consistently with confidence and authenticity.

In just a few months, people started recognizing her name. Her inbox filled with speaking requests, podcast invites, and collaboration offers. She didn't need to shout or chase anymore—her brand spoke for her. Visibility turned into credibility, and credibility turned into consistent bookings.

My Mindset Shift

I thought I'd be a writing professor forever. I loved teaching, and I was good at it. But after the pandemic, everything shifted. In 2022, my contract wasn't renewed. I was shocked. It felt like the rug had been pulled from under me.

But instead of giving up, I made a bold decision—I retired from education and went full-time into my business. That first year? No money. I lived off savings. I cried some days. But I stayed the course. Year two brought traction. And now in year three, my calendar is full and I sometimes have to turn clients away. That closed door wasn't rejection—it was redirection.

Words of Wisdom

Your message is not just what you say—it's what you *stand for*. The more you own it, the more your audience will too.

Step-by-Step Action Plan: Own Your Message, Own the Room

1. Write down five words or phrases that describe your core message.
2. Identify one story from your life that illustrates your message.
3. Create a one-sentence version of your message (this becomes your "sticky statement").
4. Practice sharing your sticky statement in conversations until it feels natural.
5. Build your next talk around that message, not the other way around

Quick Wins

- Record yourself explaining your message in under 60 seconds.
- Test your sticky statement on a friend and ask, "What did you hear me say?"
- Write three social media posts that align with your message.

- Add your message to your email signature and speaker bio.

Journal Prompt

If you had only one chance to speak to the world, what would you say—and why?

_____
_____
_____
_____

Reflection

My biggest takeaway:
_____
My next move:
_____

Key Points to Remember

- Your message is your brand.
- People can't remember what isn't clear.
- Authenticity always beats imitation.
- Clarity makes you memorable and bookable.
- Your message should solve a problem or inspire action.

Mic Drop Moment

"When you know your message, you never wonder what to say—you just stand up and speak."

Affirmation

"My message is clear. My words have impact. I speak with confidence, and my audience remembers what I stand for."

Prompt for AI

Act as a speaking coach. Create three variations of my signature message that I can use for different audiences—corporate, women's events, and online trainings.

Smart Thinking: Stop waiting to be discovered. When you show up consistently and confidently, the right people start looking for you. Visibility builds trust—and trust leads to opportunity.

Step Into the Spotlight Recap

Your brand is not your logo or colors—it's the experience people have with you. When you build your personal brand with clarity and intention, you stop being invisible and start being unforgettable. Step into the spotlight by letting your authentic voice and story shine through your brand.

Speaker's Get Paid Checklist

1. Identify your core message and write it in one clear sentence.
2. Develop a signature talk that delivers measurable outcomes.
3. Create a short version (15-20 min) and long version (45-60 min) of your talk.
4. Add your signature message to your website, speaker sheet, and social media bios.

5. Collect testimonials that highlight how your message impacted an audience.
6. Pitch yourself to at least five events this month using your signature message.
7. Practice delivering your message until you can do it confidently—without notes.

Trainings for you as you grow or scale your coaching and speaking business

Podia https://marshalynnhudson.podia.com/

Youtube https://www.youtube.com/@MarshaLynnHudson

Payhip https://payhip.com/marshalynnhudson

Newsletter https://marshalynnhudson.substack.com/

Marsha Hudson Media https://marshahudsonmedia.com/

Chapter 3

Craft a Signature Talk That Sells –
Inspire, Connect, and Open Doors to
Income

"A great talk doesn't just inspire—it creates a next step."

When people hear "signature talk," they often think about a polished speech that makes them look good. But a true signature talk is more than a performance—it's a bridge. It connects your story and expertise to the people who need it, and it leads them somewhere next. That "next" might be joining your email list, booking you for another talk, buying your book, or signing up for your program. The goal is not just applause—it's action.

When I first started speaking, I would finish my talk, thank the audience, and walk off the stage. I thought my job was done. But then I noticed something: people would say, "That was great!" and go on with their lives. My talk had inspired them, but it hadn't given them a clear next step. I realized my talk was missing the most important element— a call to action. If you want your speaking to create impact *and* income, you need a talk that moves people emotionally and directs them practically.

Embracing the power within starts with realizing that you already have what it takes to rise above any obstacle. Too often, we wait for permission, a perfect moment, or someone else to validate our worth before we take action.

The truth is, no one else can give you the kind of permission you really need—you have to give it to yourself. That means deciding that your dreams matter, your voice matters, and your life matters. It's about owning your story, including the parts you wish had gone differently. Every experience you've had has shaped the strength, wisdom, and determination you carry today. And that strength is already in you, whether you recognize it yet or not. You don't need to go looking for it—it's been there all along.

We tend to underestimate ourselves because we focus on what we haven't done instead of what we've already overcome. Think about the moments in your past when you thought you couldn't make it, but you did. Those moments are proof that you can do hard things. You've survived loss, disappointment, setbacks, and challenges you never expected. Each one has left you with a kind of grit that can't be taught—it's earned. That grit is what will carry you into the next chapter of your life. And it's why you can walk into the unknown with more confidence than you think. You've done it before, and you can do it again.

The power within you grows when you take small, consistent actions in the direction of your goals. Waiting for motivation or a burst of inspiration is risky because feelings fade. But discipline—showing up even when it's hard—builds the kind of momentum that changes everything. You don't have to have it all figured out to begin. You just have to start with what you know and learn along the way. Each step forward makes the next one easier. And over time, those small steps add up to big transformation. That's the quiet power most people overlook.

Owning your power also means setting boundaries that protect your energy and your peace. You can't pour into your purpose if you're constantly drained by distractions, negativity, or people who don't support you. Boundaries aren't about shutting people out—they're about making sure the right people and opportunities have room to come in. They allow you to focus on what matters most and say "no" to what doesn't. And saying "no" is not selfish—it's an act of self-respect. The stronger your boundaries, the stronger your ability to stay aligned with your calling. Protecting your space protects your growth.

Sometimes, tapping into your power means letting go of the version of you that can't take you where you're going. That might mean shedding old beliefs, breaking toxic patterns, or releasing relationships that no longer serve your future. It's not always easy—letting go rarely is—but it's necessary if you want to step into something greater. Every time you release what's holding you back, you make space for what can move you forward. And while the letting go might feel painful in the moment, the freedom it creates is worth it. You'll find that your true self can shine brighter without all that extra weight.

The power within isn't just about what you can do—it's about who you are becoming in the process. It's about learning to trust yourself, even when the path ahead is unclear. It's about believing that your life has purpose, even when you can't see the full picture yet. And it's about showing up for yourself every day, no matter how imperfectly. You don't have to be fearless to move forward; you just have to be willing. Willing to take the next step. Willing to bet on yourself. And willing to believe that you were made for more.

Milestone Marker

By the end of this chapter, you should have:

- Outlined your **signature talk framework** (introduction, story, teaching points, and call to action).
- Identified the one transformation your audience should walk away with.
- Practiced sharing a 5-minute version of your talk with clarity and confidence.

How Do I Write a Speech from My Framework?

If you have a framework, you already have the foundation for a powerful talk. Now it's time to turn it into a message that moves people—and sells.

Your framework is your **signature system**—the step-by-step process that leads your audience from **where they are** to **where they want to be.** It's what sets you apart. It turns your speech into a solution. Let's walk through how to craft your signature talk using your framework.

Step 1: Break Your Framework into 3–5 Core Steps

Most great frameworks are built around 3–5 pillars, phases, or shifts.
→ Examples:

- **The Success Trifecta™**: Brand. Market. Lead.
- **Power of One™**: One Person. One Offer. One Strategy.

- **The SPEAK Method**: Story. Positioning. Engagement. Action. Key Offer.

Step 2: Give Each Step a Story + Strategy

- Share a **relatable story** (yours or a client's)
- Teach 1–2 key **principles or lessons**
- Add a **visual or metaphor** if possible (e.g., ladder, toolbox, journey)

 Pro Tip: Use the phrase: *"Here's what this looked like in my life (or business)..."* then pivot to *"Here's what this can look like for you."*

Step 3: Create a Strong Opening & Closing

Opening:

- Ask a bold question
- Share a personal "this used to be me" story
- Paint a picture of what's possible for the audience

Closing:

- Reiterate your 3–5 steps
- Cast the vision: *"Imagine what your life/business could look like..."*
- Include a clear **call to action**: download, join, book, buy

What is a Signature Talk ?

Your signature talk is the one presentation you could deliver again and again to different audiences and still feel excited about. It's the talk that captures your core message, tells your most powerful stories, and delivers real transformation.

A signature talk:

- Positions you as an authority in your niche.
- Builds trust with your audience.
- Inspires action.
- Creates opportunities for bookings, partnerships, and paid offers.

When you have a solid signature talk, you stop reinventing the wheel every time you speak. You refine it, you master it, and you become known for it.

My Story: The Talk That Turned Into Clients

I once spoke at a women's networking lunch. I told my story, gave tips, and closed with a heartfelt thank-you. People loved it. But I didn't give them anywhere to go next. Six months later, I was invited to speak again—but this time, I ended by saying, "If today's message resonated with you, I'd love to stay connected. I have a free guide to help you take the next step. Just drop your email at the back table."

That day, I collected 48 email addresses. Those names turned into coaching clients, book sales, and referrals. The talk was the same, but the outcome was completely different—because I built in a clear next step. That's when

I learned a signature talk isn't just about what you say—it's about where you lead people.

The 4 Parts of a Signature Talk That Sells

1. **The Hook** – Capture attention in the first 10–30 seconds with a story, question, or bold statement.
2. **The Heart** – Share your core message and stories that connect emotionally.
3. **The How** – Give 2–4 practical takeaways the audience can use right away.
4. **The Hand-off** – Invite them to a clear next step (free resource, booking, program, or product). Don't leave your audience inspired but unsure of what to do next. Give them one clear step—download your freebie, book a call, join your program, or reflect on a prompt. This is how you move from "great talk" to *booked client*.

Prompt:

What is the ONE clear call to action you want to leave them with?

Get Paid!

A strong signature talk can become your most profitable business asset. Here's why: once your talk is dialed in, you can package it for different markets—corporate workshops, conference keynotes, community events, and online trainings. The same talk can sell over and over because you've built it to be flexible and results-driven.

You can also turn your signature talk into:

- A half-day or full-day workshop (higher fees).
- An online course or masterclass.
- A book or eBook.
- A paid group coaching program.

When you know your talk delivers value and results, it becomes easier to confidently quote your fee and stand by it. You're not selling "just a talk"—you're selling transformation.

Problem & Solution

Problem: Many speakers deliver inspiring talks that leave the audience clapping—but not acting.
Solution: Craft a talk that connects emotionally, delivers value, and ends with a clear, compelling next step.

Imagine this Scenario

She had plenty of knowledge but struggled to turn it into a message that connected. After finally crafting a signature talk with a clear structure and transformation, everything shifted.

She delivered it at a small local event, and by the end of her talk, three people approached her to book her for future engagements. One even asked if she offered coaching. That one talk became the foundation for her new business, leading to paid speaking, new clients, and online course sales. Clarity in her talk brought clarity in her business—and results followed.

My Mindset Shift

I remember early on when I would speak—whether on a Zoom, at a workshop, or in a classroom—people would always come up afterward and say, "You were the best speaker I've ever heard" or "You changed the way I think." At first, I brushed it off. But then I realized…
Every time I spoke, someone walked away empowered. That wasn't a coincidence. That was confirmation. I had something powerful inside of me—and I had a responsibility to share it.

Every time I spoke, someone walked away empowered. That wasn't a coincidence—it was a pattern. It was a sign. I had something powerful inside of me that wasn't just for me. I had a message that could move rooms, shift perspectives, and light fires. And with that came a responsibility to lead with it. I had to shift my mindset to believe I was *already* a leader. Not because I had a fancy mic or a viral video. But because when I opened my mouth—lives shifted.

Common Mistakes and How to Avoid Them

- **Mistake:** Trying to cover too much in one talk.
  Avoid it: Choose one core transformation and build around that.
- **Mistake:** Making the talk all about you.
  Avoid it: Use your story as a bridge, but make the audience the hero.
- **Mistake:** Forgetting to invite people to take the next step.
  Avoid it: Always close with a simple call to action (book a call, join your list).

Words of Wisdom

Your talk isn't just a speech—it's a system. The right structure turns applause into action and action into income.

Implementation Assignment

Write the **outline for your signature talk** today. Use this simple flow:

1. Hook (grab their attention).
2. Story (connect with your audience).
3. Teaching Points (3 key lessons).
4. Call to Action (where do they go next?).

Record yourself giving a short version, even if it's just 3–5 minutes, and watch it back to see where you can refine.

Step-by-Step Action Plan: Craft Your Signature Talk That Sells

1. Write down your core message in one sentence.
2. Outline 2–4 key points that support that message.
3. Choose 1–2 personal stories that make those points unforgettable.
4. Decide on a clear call to action (freebie, booking, product, or program).
5. Practice your talk out loud until it feels natural, not memorized.

Quick Wins

- Create a one-sheet outline of your talk with the hook, key points, and call to action.
- Record yourself delivering your talk and watch for pacing, clarity, and energy.
- Share a short version of your talk on Instagram Live or LinkedIn to test audience response.
- Write your talk's closing invitation in one strong sentence and practice saying it with confidence.

Journal Prompt

What transformation do I want my audience to experience by the end of my talk?

_____

_____

_____

Reflection

My biggest takeaway:

_____

My next move:

_____

Key Points to Remember

- Your signature talk is a bridge, not just a performance.
- The right structure turns inspiration into action.
- A clear call to action is non-negotiable.
- You can repackage one great talk into multiple income streams.
- Practice is the secret to confidence.

Mic Drop Moment

"Don't just speak to inspire—speak to move people to action."

Affirmation

"My words inspire, connect, and create opportunities. My talk changes lives—and it pays me well."

Prompt for AI

Act as a presentation coach. Give me three ways to turn my signature talk into paid workshops or courses.

Smart Thinking: A powerful talk doesn't just move hearts; it moves people to action. When you structure your story with a clear message and offer, you turn inspiration into income.

Step Into the Spotlight Recap

Your signature talk is not just a speech—it's your business card, your sales funnel, and your brand in action. When you craft a clear, repeatable talk, you create opportunities every time you speak. Step into the spotlight by preparing a talk that inspires, educates, and opens the door to paid opportunities.

Speaker's Get Paid Checklist – For Crafting a Signature Talk That Sells

1. Define your talk's core message in one clear sentence.
2. Structure your talk with a strong hook, heart, how, and hand-off.
3. Choose stories that connect emotionally and illustrate your points.
4. Build a clear call to action into your closing.
5. Create a professional one-sheet that outlines your talk.
6. Record a high-quality video of you delivering your talk.
7. Rehearse until you can deliver it confidently without notes.
8. Adapt your talk for different lengths (15 min, 30 min, 60 min).
9. Decide on your starting fee and stick to it.
10. Pitch your talk to at least five events, organizations, or conferences this month.

Chapter 4

Create a Transformation Statement & Signature Name – Give Your Talk a Powerful Identity

"When people can repeat what you do in one sentence, they can sell you without even trying."

One of the biggest reasons speakers struggle to get booked isn't because they lack talent or a great story—it's because people can't clearly explain what they do. If your talk's name and promise aren't clear, you make it hard for event planners, decision-makers, and even your own audience to recommend you. That's where your **transformation statement** and **signature name** come in. These two elements give your talk an identity. The transformation statement tells people exactly what result or change your audience will experience. The signature name makes your talk memorable and marketable. Together, they become your calling card in the speaking world.

Overcoming limiting beliefs begins with recognizing that they are just thoughts, not facts. Too many of us treat the stories we've told ourselves for years as if they are absolute truth. These beliefs often come from past experiences, things people have said, or fears we've carried since childhood. But they are not the full picture of who you are or what you're capable of.

A limiting belief might whisper, "You're not ready," or "You're not good enough," but those are just echoes of the past. You have the power to replace them with a new story that reflects your potential instead of your fears. The first step is noticing when these thoughts show up and questioning whether they're really true. Often, you'll find that they don't stand up to the truth of your resilience.

Limiting beliefs are sneaky because they can hide in your daily habits and decisions. They show up when you hesitate to take a chance, when you downplay your talents, or when you stay in situations that don't serve you. Sometimes they sound reasonable, like "I just don't have time," when in reality, you're afraid of what might happen if you fully commit. By becoming aware of these patterns, you can start to interrupt them. Every time you challenge a limiting belief, you take away some of its power. And each time you choose courage over fear, you strengthen your confidence. This is how transformation begins—one belief at a time.

One of the most effective ways to break through limiting beliefs is to take action, even if you don't feel ready. Action creates evidence, and evidence changes your mindset. When you try something and see that you can do it, you start to believe it's possible. That's why waiting for confidence before you act will keep you stuck. Confidence doesn't come first—it comes from doing the thing you thought you couldn't do. Each small win builds a stronger foundation for the next step. And over time, those steps can take you farther than you ever imagined.

Another powerful tool for overcoming limiting beliefs is surrounding yourself with people who see your potential. The right environment can help you rise higher because it reinforces the belief that you are capable. Sometimes you need someone else to remind you of your greatness when you can't see it yourself. This doesn't mean you need constant validation—it means you need voices of truth that speak louder than your inner critic. Seek out mentors, friends, and communities that inspire and challenge you. Let their belief in you help bridge the gap until your own belief catches up. And when it does, you'll have a new strength that no old story can shake.

Rewriting your beliefs also means speaking to yourself in a new way. The words you repeat daily become the beliefs you live by. If you constantly tell yourself you're behind, unqualified, or not ready, your actions will follow that script. But if you start speaking life into your dreams— saying, "I am capable, I am prepared, I am worthy"—your mindset will shift. Positive self-talk is not about pretending everything is perfect; it's about choosing a perspective that moves you forward. Over time, these words will feel natural, and the old limiting beliefs will fade into the background. What you say to yourself matters more than you realize.

The truth is, your potential is not determined by the limits you've believed in the past. It's determined by the limits you're willing to release today. Every time you let go of a belief that keeps you small, you create more room for growth, opportunity, and purpose. You don't have to change everything overnight; you just have to start with one thought, one choice, one step. As you keep moving, you'll find that your life expands to match the new beliefs you've embraced. And once you see what's possible, you'll never want to go back to the old way of thinking. That's the freedom that comes from breaking through the walls in your mind.

Milestone Marker

By the end of this chapter, you should have:

- Written a clear **transformation statement** that communicates the results you help create.
- Chosen a **signature name** for your talk that is memorable and marketable.
- Practiced introducing yourself using your transformation statement with confidence.

Why This Matters More Than You Think

Event planners are busy. They need to know—in seconds—what you speak about, why it matters, and how it will help their audience. If they can't "see it" right away, they'll move on to the next speaker.

Think about it:

- A vague talk title like *Empower Your Life* doesn't tell anyone what they'll walk away with.
- A transformation statement like *Helping women go from fear to fearless so they can step into their calling with confidence* instantly paints a picture. Clarity is what gets you booked.

My Story: The Pitch That Fell Flat

Years ago, I pitched myself for a corporate women's event. My talk title was something like *Living Your Best Life*. It sounded nice—but it was generic. They passed on me and hired another speaker. A few months later, I saw her presentation title: *From Burnout to Breakthrough: Three Strategies to Reclaim Your Energy and Lead With Impact.*

The difference? Her title told them exactly what the audience would get. Mine sounded like something they'd heard a hundred times before. That experience changed how I approach naming my talks. I stopped being vague and started getting specific.

How to Create Your Transformation Statement

Your transformation statement should answer these two questions:

1. Who is the talk for?
2. What change will they experience by the end?

Formula: **I help [audience] go from [starting point] to [end result] so they can [big benefit].**

Examples:

- "I help women entrepreneurs go from overwhelmed to organized so they can grow their business without burnout."
- "I help emerging leaders go from unsure to confident so they can lead with authority and inspire their teams."

How to Create a Signature Name

Your talk's name should be:

- **Clear:** Easy to understand without explanation.
- **Catchy:** Something people will remember.
- **Compelling:** It hints at a result or benefit.

Ideas:

- Use contrast: *From Fear to Fearless*
- Promise a benefit: *The Confidence Blueprint*
- Be specific: *Five Steps to Building a Brand That Books You*

Implementation Assignment

- Write your transformation statement using this formula:
  "I help [specific audience] go from [current struggle] to [desired outcome]."
- Then, brainstorm three possible titles for your talk. Share them with a trusted friend or colleague and choose the one that feels strong, clear, and memorable.

Get Paid!

A great transformation statement and signature name don't just help you get booked—they help you get paid more. Why? Because when decision-makers clearly understand the outcome and value of your talk, they can justify paying you. When your talk is marketable, you become easier to recommend. Your title can be shared in an email, a meeting, or even over coffee—and that means more referrals. And when your transformation statement shows measurable impact, organizations see you as a problem-solver, not just a motivational speaker. Problem-solvers get bigger budgets.

Problem & Solution

Problem: Many speakers have generic talk titles and unclear promises, making it hard for others to recommend or hire them.
Solution: Create a clear, outcome-driven transformation statement and a memorable signature name so your talk sells itself.

Imagine this Scenario

She used to fumble when people asked, "So, what do you do?" Her response changed every time—and so did people's interest. Once she created a clear transformation statement and gave her talk a signature name, things clicked.

Suddenly, people remembered her. They repeated her phrase when introducing her. Event organizers started saying, "We need that topic at our event." Her new message positioned her as an expert. It opened the door to collaborations, podcast interviews, and even a training contract with a local organization—all because she could clearly state the value she delivered.

My Mindset Shift

I used to think selling was pushy.
I didn't want to "pitch" or sound like one of those online gurus with a flashy promise and a countdown timer. I just wanted to *help people.* So for a long time, I held back. I shared my content, gave away free value, and waited for people to reach out. But here's the truth: **most people need an invitation.** They need to be *told* what the next step is,

and they want to feel confident that investing in you is the right move.

Once I stopped looking at selling as "asking for money" and started seeing it as **offering transformation**, everything shifted. Now when I speak, teach, or post, I *always* make an offer — with heart, clarity, and confidence. And people respond with a "yes" because the energy is different. It's not pressure. It's purpose. Selling isn't sleazy when it's aligned. It's a service.

Common Mistakes and How to Avoid Them

- **Mistake:** Using vague language that doesn't show results.
  Avoid it: Be clear about the transformation—what changes for the audience after they hear you?
- **Mistake:** Having a talk title that's too generic.
  Avoid it: Create a title that's specific, bold, and easy to remember.
- **Mistake:** Making the statement all about you.
  Avoid it: Focus on what you help *them* achieve

Words of Wisdom

Your talk's name isn't just a title—it's your marketing hook. The clearer and more compelling it is, the easier it is for people to say "yes."

Step-by-Step Action Plan: Create Your Transformation Statement & Signature Name

1. Write down your ideal audience.
2. Identify the starting point of your audience (their struggle or challenge).

3. Identify the end result (what they want most).
4. Fill in the formula: I help [audience] go from [starting point] to [end result] so they can [big benefit].
5. Brainstorm 5–10 possible names for your talk and choose the one that is clearest and most compelling.

Quick Wins

- Test your transformation statement on a friend—ask them to repeat it back to you.
- Post your talk title on social media and see which one gets the most engagement.
- Add your transformation statement to your speaker bio and pitch emails.
- Update your website with your new talk title and statement.

Journal Prompt

If I could promise my audience one transformation by the end of my talk, what would it be?

_____

_____

_____

Reflection

My biggest takeaway:

_____

My next move:

_____

Key Points to Remember

- Clarity gets you booked.
- A transformation statement makes your promise clear.
- A signature name makes your talk memorable.
- Specificity beats vague, every time.
- Your talk's title and statement are marketing tools—use them.

Mic Drop Moment

"If you can't explain what you do in one sentence, you're making it too hard for people to hire you."

Affirmation

"My message is clear, my talk is unforgettable, and decision-makers can't wait to book me."

Prompt for AI

Act as a speaking coach. Create three transformation statements and matching signature talk names for my audience of women entrepreneurs.

Smart Thinking: Don't make people guess what you do. Speak with confidence and let your transformation statement become your business card, your elevator pitch, and your mission.

Step Into the Spotlight Recap

A transformation statement and signature name are more than just words—they are your brand's heartbeat. They help people remember you, share your message, and book you. Step into the spotlight by making your message unforgettable with clarity and confidence.

Speaker's Get Paid Checklist

1. Define your audience clearly.
2. Write your transformation statement using the "from-to-so they can" formula.
3. Brainstorm 5–10 possible talk names that are clear, catchy, and benefit-driven.
4. Choose one talk name and test it with your target audience.
5. Add your talk name and transformation statement to your website and speaker sheet.
6. Include your transformation statement in all pitch emails.
7. Practice introducing your talk in conversation in 20 seconds or less.
8. Use your talk's name consistently so you become known for it.
9. Align your social media posts and marketing with your transformation statement.
10. Pitch your newly branded talk to five decision-makers this month.

Trainings for you as you grow or scale your coaching and speaking business

Podia https://marshalynnhudson.podia.com/

Youtube https://www.youtube.com/@MarshaLynnHudson

Payhip https://payhip.com/marshalynnhudson

Newsletter https://marshalynnhudson.substack.com/

Marsha Hudson Media https://marshahudsonmedia.com/

https://www.facebook.com/groups/femaleentrepreneurswho
buildbusinessesonline- facebook group

Chapter 5

Turn Your Ideas into Income with a Lead Magnet Suite – Keep the Conversation Going After the Applause

"The real money isn't in the talk—it's in what happens after."

One of the biggest mistakes speakers make is thinking the stage is the end of the journey. You give a powerful talk, people clap, you thank them, and you walk away. But here's the truth—if you leave without giving your audience a way to stay connected, you're walking away from potential clients, customers, and income. A great talk is the spark. A **lead magnet suite** is the bridge that turns that spark into a relationship, and eventually, into revenue.

You don't need a perfect plan to get started, but you do need a decision. Too many people stay stuck because they're waiting for the "right time," the "right resources," or the "right coach." The truth is, clarity comes from movement. You won't figure it all out by thinking — you'll figure it out by doing. That's how I moved forward. I didn't have all the answers, but I had the willingness to learn and the commitment to take one step each day. That's how momentum is built. And once momentum kicks in, confidence follows.

If you're trying to build a business, brand, or even a new season in your life — you need to give yourself permission to grow in the process. Stop comparing your day one to someone else's year five. That mindset will drain your energy and kill your creativity. Your lane is powerful when you stay in it. Focus on who you are, who you want to become, and how you want to show up. That's the foundation of authentic leadership. You can build something real, but it has to start with owning your story and your vision. That's where your power lives.

This journey isn't about being busy — it's about being aligned. I had to learn that lesson the hard way. I used to fill my days with tasks, but not results. I was "working," but not growing. That's why structure and intention became non-negotiable for me. When you set clear goals and map your days around them, you reclaim your time and energy. That's when you stop running in circles and start making real progress. That's what alignment looks like.

People often ask me, "How do I stay consistent?" And I always say — make it easier to win. Set up a system that supports your success, not sabotages it. That means stop overthinking content, simplify your offers, and make your marketing repeatable. Consistency comes from simplicity, not complexity. It's not about doing more — it's about doing what works, over and over again. When you build routines that feel doable, you'll show up more, and show up better. That's how you win.

You don't need to be everywhere to be effective. Pick two platforms and show up intentionally. One of the biggest shifts I made was giving myself permission to simplify. I stopped chasing trends and started building trust. My audience grew because I was clear, not because I was flashy. You don't have to go viral to be valuable. Focus on connection, not just content. And remember, your energy is your brand — people feel it before they hear your message.

Lastly, keep in mind: this is your race. There's no deadline on your dream. You're not behind, you're just building. I want to remind you that small steps still count. You don't need a massive breakthrough — you need daily belief. Trust yourself, trust your process, and trust that the vision you have is worth the effort. I'm cheering for you, and I'm proof that this kind of growth is possible. Let's keep building.

Milestone Marker

By the end of this chapter, you should have:

- Chosen one **lead magnet idea** (checklist, guide, or mini-training).
- Created a simple outline or draft of that lead magnet.
- Identified how your lead magnet connects directly to your signature talk.

Why You Need a Lead Magnet Suite

Your audience is most excited about you in the moments right after you speak. That's when your message is fresh in their minds and their emotions are high. If you don't have a way for them to stay in your world, you lose the momentum you just created.

A **lead magnet suite** is simply a set of free or low-cost offers that capture people's contact information, give them value, and lead them toward your paid offers. It keeps the conversation going long after the event is over.

My Story: The Day I Learned the Power of the "Next Step"

I once spoke at a conference where I gave one of my best talks ever. The audience was fired up. People were nodding, taking notes, and even wiping away tears. But when it ended, I didn't offer anything. No free guide, no sign-up sheet, no follow-up.

A few weeks later, I realized something—out of 75 people in that room, not one of them had a way to hear from me again. That's 75 lost connections, and potentially thousands of dollars in lost revenue.

I made a promise to myself right then: never again would I leave a stage without offering a clear, valuable next step. And when I did, everything changed.

What Goes in a Lead Magnet Suite?

Think of your lead magnet suite as a menu. Not everyone will want the same thing, so give them options:

- **Quick Win Freebie:** A checklist, PDF guide, or short video they can use right away.
- **Deep Dive Resource:** A free webinar, audio training, or mini-course that builds more trust.
- **Low-Cost Offer:** A $17–$47 product that gives value and introduces them to your paid world.

The key is to make it easy to say yes. Your audience should be able to sign up right there in the room or online—no complicated steps, no confusion.

How This Ties to Your Speaking

Every time you speak, your lead magnet suite should be part of your plan. Your closing should include something like:

"If today's message resonated with you, I've created a free resource to help you take the next step. Just scan this QR code or visit this link, and I'll send it right to your inbox."

This does two things:

1. Positions you as someone who provides ongoing value, not just a one-time talk.
2. Builds your email list so you can continue the relationship and eventually make offers.

Implementation Assignment

> Choose one idea for your first lead magnet. Write down the title and the three main points it will cover. Create a simple draft (no more than 2–3 pages if it's written). Share it with a friend or colleague to test if it feels valuable and clear.

Get Paid!

Here's where it gets exciting—a lead magnet suite doesn't just grow your list, it grows your income. Every time someone downloads your freebie or buys your low-cost offer, they enter your ecosystem. From there, you can invite them into higher-ticket programs, workshops, masterminds, or one-on-one coaching. Your speaking fee is one revenue stream. Your lead magnet suite creates multiple streams.

This is how you turn a one-day speaking opportunity into long-term income.

Problem & Solution

Problem: Most speakers inspire people but have no system to keep the connection alive after the event.
Solution: Create a lead magnet suite that captures contact information, nurtures relationships, and leads to paid offers.

Imagine this Scenario

She started with one signature talk at a women's networking event. Inspired by the message, attendees asked, "Do you have something I can download?" That question sparked her lead magnet suite—she created a simple checklist, followed by a workbook, then a mini course.

Within 60 days, her one talk turned into three digital products and a coaching offer. Her email list grew. She began booking discovery calls from her lead magnet thank-you page. What started as "just a talk" became a full income-generating ecosystem—and she didn't need a big team or fancy tech.

My Mindset Shift

For a long time, I thought the "stage" meant a conference with lights, rows of chairs, and a big microphone. So I waited for someone to invite me up there. But guess what?

The stage was already mine.

When I went live on Instagram, that was a stage. When I recorded a podcast, that was a stage.
When I posted a message on LinkedIn that resonated with someone—that was a stage too. I had been overlooking the platforms I already had access to because I didn't think they counted. But the truth is, **your stage is wherever your message meets someone who needs it.**

Once I embraced that, I stopped shrinking. I showed up boldly—online, offline, on Zoom, in emails, everywhere. And every time I shared my message intentionally, it opened a door: a client, an opportunity, a contract. Don't wait to be chosen. **Choose yourself.**

Common Mistakes and How to Avoid Them

- **Mistake:** Creating a complicated or overly long lead magnet.
  Avoid it: Keep it short, actionable, and tied to your talk's transformation.
- **Mistake:** Offering something that doesn't lead to your paid offer.
  Avoid it: Make sure your lead magnet flows naturally into your program, coaching, or workshop.
- **Mistake:** Creating too many freebies at once.
  Avoid it: Start with one solid lead magnet and build from there.

Words of Wisdom

Your talk is the front door. Your lead magnet suite is the house. Don't invite people to the party and forget to let them in.

Step-by-Step Action Plan: Build Your Lead Magnet Suite

1. Decide on one quick win freebie your audience will love.
2. Create one deeper resource that positions you as the expert.
3. Add one low-cost offer to give them a way to invest in you right away.
4. Set up a simple landing page and delivery system for each.
5. Practice weaving your lead magnet into your talk's closing.

Quick Wins

- Brainstorm three quick win freebie ideas and choose one to create this week.
- Create a QR code that links directly to your freebie sign-up page.
- Write a 30-second script for offering your freebie at the end of your talk.
- Add your freebie link to your slides, handouts, and email signature.

Journal Prompt

What resource could I create that would help my audience take immediate action on my message?

_____
_____
_____

Reflection

My biggest takeaway:

_____

My next move:

_____

Key Points to Remember

- The audience is most engaged immediately after your talk.
- A lead magnet suite keeps you in their world.
- Offering value after the talk builds trust and authority.
- Multiple entry points lead to multiple income streams.
- Speaking without a follow-up plan is leaving money on the table.

Mic Drop Moment

"The applause will fade, but the relationship can last for years—if you have a way to keep it alive."

Affirmation

"I always give my audience a way to stay connected, and my message continues to work long after I leave the stage."

Prompt for AI

Act as a marketing strategist. Create three lead magnet suite ideas for a speaker who teaches women entrepreneurs how to grow their business.

Smart Thinking: Build a system around one talk, one message, and one transformation. Let your lead magnet work behind the scenes to attract and nurture your audience while you focus on showing up with purpose.

Step Into the Spotlight Recap

Your lead magnet is the bridge between inspiration and action. It's what helps you keep the connection alive after the applause. Step into the spotlight by turning your ideas into income—one lead magnet at a time.

Speaker's Get Paid Checklist

1. Identify your audience's most urgent problem and create a quick win freebie.
2. Develop a deeper resource that builds more trust (webinar, audio training, or mini-course).
3. Add a low-cost offer to introduce your paid products or services.
4. Set up an easy sign-up process with a QR code and landing page.
5. Add your lead magnet links to your talk slides and closing script.
6. Practice delivering your offer naturally during your talk.
7. Have a follow-up email sequence ready to nurture new leads.
8. Track how many sign-ups you get from each event.
9. Test different freebies to see which ones convert best.
10. Use your lead magnet suite at every speaking engagement—no exceptions.

PART TWO: BUILD YOUR STAGE PRESENCE

6. Build Your Online Presence with Intention
Position yourself as the go-to expert in your space.

7. Turn Your Talk into a Value Ladder
Transform one message into multiple offers, programs, and products.

8. Grow Your Email List from Zero
Use talks, social media, and lead magnets to grow your audience.

9. Master the Discovery Call
Convert conversations into clients—without being pushy.

10. Keep Learning, Keep Earning
How continuous growth fuels speaking, coaching, and course opportunities.

11. Speaker Toolkit: Get Booked with Ease
What to include in your reel, media kit, and pitch for more yeses.

Chapter 6

Build Your Online Presence with

Intention – Be Seen, Be Heard, Be Booked

"If you're not showing up online, you're invisible to the people who need you."

You've laid your foundation—you've faced the fear, owned your message, crafted your talk, and created ways for people to keep connecting with you after the applause. Now it's time for the next step: making sure the world *sees* you.

In today's world, your online presence is your stage before you ever step on a physical one. Event planners, decision-makers, and audience members will look you up before they ever hire you, follow you, or book you. What they see—or don't see—can make or break your speaking opportunities.

There are moments in life that will bring you to your knees — loss, heartbreak, failure, disappointment. I've been there, and I know how it feels to smile in public while silently hurting. But here's what I learned: healing isn't about pretending everything is fine. Healing is about giving yourself permission to feel and still move forward. It's about choosing growth even when pain is still sitting at the table. You don't have to rush your process. You don't have to explain your healing to anyone. But you do have to choose yourself again — and again.

Pain has a way of revealing your strength. You don't realize how much power you carry until you're forced to rise when everything around you feels like it's falling apart. I've discovered that my greatest breakthroughs came from my lowest valleys. It wasn't the easy days that made me stronger — it was the ones that nearly broke me. Loss will come. Disappointment will come. But what matters most is how you rise. You can lose a lot, and still not lose yourself.

Letting go is one of the hardest things to do. Whether it's a person, a season, a mistake, or even an old version of you — it takes courage. But holding on to what's hurting you keeps you stuck. I had to learn that letting go doesn't mean giving up. It means clearing space for something better. It means allowing peace to enter where pain once lived. And it means trusting that what's ahead is more aligned than what's behind.

Grief doesn't follow a timeline. And healing isn't linear. Some days you'll feel powerful, and some days you'll feel like you're back at square one. Both are normal. What's important is that you don't shame yourself for how you feel. Give yourself grace. Celebrate the small wins. And remember, you're allowed to be both healing and hopeful at the same time.

The past may have shaped you, but it does not define you. You are not your mistakes. You are not what happened to you. You are who you choose to become next. That choice is where your freedom lives. Every time you speak life over yourself, you rewrite the narrative. Every time you show up again, you reclaim your story. Your pain has purpose — and your story has power.

As you move forward, take the lessons with you but leave the weight behind. Carry the wisdom, not the wounds. You deserve to live light. You deserve peace. And even if you've walked through fire, you're still standing — stronger, wiser, more ready than ever. You're not behind. You're becoming. And that's more than enough.

Milestone Marker

By the end of this chapter, you should have:

- Audited your current online presence (Google yourself, check your profiles).
- Updated at least one profile to clearly communicate who you are and what you do.
- Identified 2 platforms where you'll commit to showing up consistently.

Your Digital Footprint: Is It Helping or Hurting Your Brand?

Every post you share, every bio you write, every platform you're on—it all leaves a trail. That trail is called your **digital footprint**, and whether you realize it or not, it's either **opening doors** or **quietly closing them**.

When someone Googles your name or clicks your LinkedIn, what do they see? Is your brand clear? Is your message consistent? Or is there confusion, clutter, or crickets?

This is where many women get stuck. You may be showing up—but you're not showing up **strategically**.

What Is Your Digital Footprint?

Your digital footprint is the collection of everything that represents you online, including:

- Your social media profiles (LinkedIn, Instagram, Facebook, YouTube, etc.)
- Your website or speaker page
- Your podcast or guest interviews
- Articles you've written or been featured in
- Your lead magnets, email signature, and online comments

These are your **first impressions at scale**. In many cases, people will form an opinion about your brand **before** they ever hear you speak.

Why You Must Check It Now

- If your bio doesn't match your message, people get confused.
- If your content is outdated or off-brand, you lose credibility.
- If people can't clearly understand what you offer, they move on.

You only get seconds to make that first digital impression. So let's make sure it reflects the expert and leader you truly are.

Quick Digital Footprint Checklist

Use this to do a mini-audit of your brand presence online.

- Does your bio clearly state who you are and what you help people do?
- Are your brand photos consistent across platforms?
- Are your posts aligned with your current message and offers?
- Is your LinkedIn banner or website up to date?
- Is it clear what your audience should do next (e.g., book you, download something, contact you)?

If you answered **no** to even one of these—don't panic. This is your opportunity to realign and upgrade.

Why "Showing Up" Online Matters

You can be the most incredible speaker in the world, but if people can't find you, they can't book you. Your online presence is often your first impression, and in the speaking world, first impressions matter.

Here's the truth:

- Event planners will Google you.
- Potential clients will check your social media.
- Your audience will follow you to stay connected.

If your online presence is unclear, inconsistent, or nonexistent, you lose credibility before you even get a chance to speak.

My Story: The Silent Opportunity I Lost

I'll never forget the time I found out I was *this close* to getting booked for a corporate event—but I lost it because my online presence didn't match the impression I made in person. The organizer told me, "We couldn't find a professional speaker page or any video clips of you." I had done the hard work in the room, but I hadn't backed it up online. That was my wake-up call. From that day on, I made it a priority to make sure my digital footprint matched the level of excellence I delivered on stage.

The 3 C's of an Intentional Online Presence

1. **Clarity** – Your bio, photos, and content should make it obvious what you do and who you help.
2. **Consistency** – Your message and visuals should be aligned across all platforms (website, LinkedIn, Instagram, etc.).
3. **Credibility** – Showcase proof of your expertise— videos, testimonials, press features, or past speaking engagements.

My 3-2-1 Framework for Staying Visible

The biggest challenge speakers face online isn't always *knowing* they need to show up—it's staying consistent without feeling overwhelmed. That's why I created my simple **3-2-1 framework** to keep your presence intentional and sustainable.

- **3** – Create three quality posts each week that position you as an expert. These could be tips, short videos, behind-the-scenes stories, or speaking clips.

- **2** – Focus on two social media platforms where your audience actually hangs out. No need to be everywhere—just be present where it matters.
- **1** – Send one email a week to your list. Stay connected, provide value, and invite them to work with you.

When you stick to 3-2-1, you build trust, visibility, and authority without burning out. It's not about posting constantly—it's about showing up with intention.

How to Make Your Online Presence Work for You

- **Your Website**: Create a simple speaker page with your bio, signature talk titles, transformation statements, and a way to contact you.
- **Social Media**: Post regularly (using the 3-2-1 framework), share clips from your talks, and create content that aligns with your message.
- **Video Content**: Even a 60-second clip of you speaking can boost your credibility instantly.
- **Professional Photos**: Invest in high-quality headshots that match your personal brand.

Get Paid!

When your online presence is intentional, it becomes a silent sales tool. People can find you, see your expertise, and decide to hire you—sometimes without you even having a conversation yet.

Think about it: if a decision-maker is choosing between two speakers—one with a polished website, a consistent brand, and speaking clips, and one with nothing but a basic profile—the first one will almost always get the booking *and* the higher fee.

Problem & Solution

Problem: Many speakers miss opportunities because their online presence is outdated, unclear, or nonexistent.
Solution: Build an intentional, consistent, and credible online presence, using the 3-2-1 framework, that works for you 24/7.

Imagine this Scenario

She used to post online sporadically with no clear message or plan. Her brand felt like a mix of quotes, random selfies, and business tips. But once she got clear on her message and built her online presence with intention—everything shifted. She updated her bios, clarified her audience, and began showing up with consistent value tied to her signature talk. Within weeks, people started reaching out asking how to work with her. Her content began attracting invitations to speak on podcasts and teach in virtual summits. The right message + the right platform = visibility and momentum.

My Mindset Shift

For a long time, I played small. I thought if I just stayed "consistent," the right people would find me. But showing up without *intention* is not the same as building *presence*. It wasn't until I started owning my space—speaking boldly, showing up confidently, and sharing my value without apology—that things shifted. I stopped waiting to be discovered and decided to *be seen*.I learned that people don't just buy what you offer—they buy how you make them feel. And when you show up with clarity, confidence, and purpose, *you become unforgettable*.

Common Mistakes and How to Avoid Them

- **Mistake:** Trying to post everywhere with no strategy.
  Avoid it: Focus on 2 platforms that align with your audience and show up consistently.
- **Mistake:** Having profiles that don't match your brand.
  Avoid it: Use the same headshot, bio, and messaging across platforms for consistency.
- **Mistake:** Sharing random content with no connection to your core message.
  Avoid it: Create posts that point back to your expertise, your talk, and your offers.

Words of Wisdom

Your online presence is not just marketing—it's positioning. It tells people you're a professional who takes their message seriously.

Step-by-Step Action Plan: Build Your Online Presence with Intention

1. Audit your current online presence—search your name and see what comes up.
2. Update your bios on all platforms to clearly state who you help and how.
3. Create or update your speaker page with your bio, topics, and contact form.
4. Post three pieces of content this week using the 3-2-1 framework.

5. Ask a past client or audience member for a testimonial and post it online.

Quick Wins

- Add your lead magnet link to your social media bios.
- Pin a post or video that introduces you to your audience.
- Upload a speaking clip to LinkedIn and tag the event host.
- Create a branded email signature with your website and social links.

Journal Prompt

If someone searched for me online right now, what impression would they get?

_____

_____

_____

Reflection

My biggest takeaway:

_____

My next move:

_____

Key Points to Remember

- Your online presence is your first stage.
- Clarity, consistency, and credibility build trust before you ever speak.
- The 3-2-1 framework keeps you visible without burnout.
- A strong digital footprint helps you book more gigs and charge more.

Mic Drop Moment

"Your online presence is speaking for you—make sure it's saying the right thing."

Affirmation

"My online presence reflects my expertise and attracts the opportunities I'm meant for."

Prompt for AI

Act as a brand strategist. Create a 30-day content plan for a speaker using the 3-2-1 framework to position themselves as a go-to expert on LinkedIn and Instagram.

Smart Thinking: Build a system around one talk, one message, and one transformation. Let your lead magnet work behind the scenes to attract and nurture your audience while you focus on showing up with purpose.

Implementation Assignment

Audit your online presence today. Google your name and take notes on what shows up. Then update one profile or your website bio to clearly reflect your message and transformation statement.

Step Into the Spotlight Recap

Your online presence is your stage before the stage. When people look you up, they should see clarity, credibility, and consistency. Step into the spotlight by making your digital footprint intentional—it will open doors before you even walk into the room.

Speaker's Get Paid Checklist – For Building Your Online Presence

1. Google your name and see what appears—note what needs updating.
2. Update all bios to clearly state your audience and transformation.
3. Create or update your speaker page with topics, testimonials, and a booking link.
4. Implement the 3-2-1 framework: 3 posts per week, 2 main platforms, 1 email weekly.
5. Share at least one speaking clip publicly.
6. Use consistent photos and branding across platforms.
7. Add a lead magnet link to all social media bios.
8. Collect and post testimonials regularly.
9. Create a short intro video for your website and social media.
10. Review your online presence quarterly to ensure it's current and aligned.

Chapter 7

Turn Your Talk into a Value Ladder –

From One Message to Multiple Offers

"Your talk isn't just a presentation—it's a pathway to your offers."

Most speakers stop at the talk. They deliver an amazing message, get the applause, maybe even collect a few business cards—and that's it. But here's the truth: your talk can be the starting point of a complete customer journey. And when you structure that journey intentionally, you create a **value ladder** that turns inspiration into action, action into conversations, and conversations into cash.

What a Value Ladder Is and Why It Works

A value ladder is a simple way to guide people from first discovering you to becoming paying clients or customers. Each step offers more value, more transformation, and often a higher price point.

Think of it like this: your audience takes small, low-risk steps toward working with you before they take the big leap into your higher-priced offers. This builds trust, credibility, and connection along the way.

My Story: How I Learned to Climb the Ladder

When I first started speaking, I thought the goal was to book *another* talk. That was my only measure of success.

But I started to realize that the stage could be the entry point into a whole ecosystem of offers.

Once I built my first value ladder, things changed. I went from one-off speaking fees to turning events into a stream of leads for my workshops, coaching programs, and digital products. And here's the thing—it wasn't complicated. It was just intentional.

Purpose doesn't always arrive wrapped in clarity. Sometimes it reveals itself through pain, detours, and even the things we didn't choose. I used to think purpose was some big, dramatic moment — but I've learned that it's often found in the quiet places of our lives. It's in the stories we carry, the people we help, and the decisions we make to keep going when quitting would be easier. Purpose is not a destination — it's a journey of becoming. You don't find it all at once. You uncover it little by little as you say yes to growth. And every step you've taken, even the missteps, are all part of the assignment.

Sometimes, what feels like a delay is really divine alignment. You're not late. You're not off track. You're being positioned. There were things you had to go through, people you had to meet, and lessons you had to learn before your purpose could unfold. I've had seasons that made no sense in the moment but made perfect sense in hindsight. And now I see — nothing was wasted. Not the tears, not the struggle, not the waiting.

Discovering your purpose often requires releasing your comfort zone. It's easy to stay where it's familiar, but growth doesn't happen in safety. I had to let go of old titles, outdated beliefs, and fear of what others would think. That's when I started stepping into something deeper. Purpose stretches you. It invites you to live beyond survival and into significance. It asks you to stop hiding and start honoring the gifts inside you.

Your purpose is connected to people. It's not just about you — it's about who you're called to help, heal, teach, or reach. When you show up, you give others permission to do the same. Your courage becomes someone else's inspiration. Your story becomes someone else's roadmap. So don't minimize your voice. What you carry is needed. Someone is waiting on the other side of your obedience.

Clarity comes in the doing. You don't have to have it all figured out to begin. Start with what you know. Serve with what you have. Use what's in your hands right now. Take the next right step — and then the one after that. You'll be surprised how purpose meets you along the way. And one day, you'll look back and realize — you were walking in purpose all along.

Living in purpose doesn't mean life will always be easy, but it will always be meaningful. Even on the hard days, you'll know that what you're doing matters. That your presence, your voice, your impact — it all counts. Keep showing up. Keep trusting the process. You're not lost. You're being led. And your purpose is unfolding right on time.

Milestone Marker

By the end of this chapter, you should have:

- Outlined how your **signature talk** can lead to at least 3 offers (free, mid-level, and premium).
- Identified one way to repurpose your talk into a program, workshop, or digital product.

- Drafted a simple next-step pathway for your audience after hearing you speak.

The Value Ladder in Action

Here's one example of how you can take one talk and turn it into a complete client journey:

1. **Lead Magnet** – At the end of your talk, offer a free resource that connects directly to your topic (PDF, checklist, mini-guide, audio training). Use a QR code or short link so it's easy to sign up.
2. **Content** – Stay visible and provide value with posts, videos, and tips that align with your message. This builds familiarity and keeps you top of mind.
3. **Email Nurture** – Send a short series of emails after they grab your freebie. Share stories, give practical tips, and let them see your personality and expertise.
4. **Show Up with a Webinar, Workshop, or Live** – Invite them to a deeper experience with you—online or in person. This is where you can teach, interact, and build more trust.
5. **Discovery or Sales Call** – For your higher-ticket offers, invite interested people to a call. Here's where conversations turn into clients.

Conversations = Cash. Every step of this ladder moves people closer to working with you—and every rung is an opportunity to serve and sell at the same time.

Why This is a Game-Changer for Speakers

When you build a value ladder, you stop relying on one-time speaking fees. Instead, every audience you speak to becomes a potential stream of new clients and customers. You can turn one talk into:

- Paid workshops and trainings
- Digital courses and products
- Coaching or consulting programs
- Long-term partnerships

Get Paid!

Event organizers may only pay you once, but the people in your audience can become clients for months or years to come. A clear value ladder means you're never walking off a stage empty-handed. Even free speaking gigs can become profitable when you know how to move people up your ladder.

Problem & Solution

Problem: Many speakers leave the stage without giving the audience a path to work with them further.
Solution: Create a value ladder that starts with a free offer and ends with your higher-ticket programs, guiding people step by step to becoming clients.

Imagine this Scenario

She started with one powerful talk that lit up the room. But instead of letting it end there, she repurposed it. That single message became a free lead magnet, a group coaching program, a digital course, and even a corporate workshop.

By strategically building her value ladder, she stopped chasing one-time opportunities and started creating multiple income streams from one signature message. Her audience grew, her income stabilized, and her impact multiplied—all from that one talk.

Mindset Shift

For years, I felt like I had to constantly come up with something new—new talks, new freebies, new offers. I didn't realize the real power was in going deeper, not wider. Once I leaned into my core message and created layers around it, I stopped spinning my wheels and started scaling. That one talk that lit a fire in the room? It became the foundation of a lead magnet, a digital course, and a signature program. I didn't need more content. I needed more *clarity* and *strategy*. **The truth? You already have enough.** Now it's time to build around it—intentionally.

Common Mistakes and How to Avoid Them

- **Mistake:** Treating your talk as a one-and-done event.
  Avoid it: Think of it as the top of your funnel that feeds into other offers.
- **Mistake:** Offering too many random products.
  Avoid it: Build a clear ladder where each step naturally leads to the next.
- **Mistake:** Forgetting to guide the audience to the next step.
  Avoid it: Always tell them where to go next—download, join, or book.

Words of Wisdom

Your talk is the introduction, not the end. The value ladder is how you keep the relationship alive—and turn interest into income.

Step-by-Step Action Plan: Build Your Value Ladder

1. Decide on a lead magnet that connects directly to your signature talk.
2. Create a simple follow-up email sequence that gives more value.
3. Plan a free or low-cost workshop, webinar, or live session.
4. Identify your higher-ticket offer and who it's for.
5. Practice inviting people to the next step during your talk.

Quick Wins

- Write your "freebie invitation" script for the end of your talk.
- Create a landing page for your lead magnet.
- Outline three nurture emails you can send after they sign up.
- Schedule a live Q&A or workshop within 30 days of your next talk.

Journal Prompt

How could I turn my current talk into a complete client journey?

_____
_____
_____

Reflection

My biggest takeaway:

_____

My next move:

_____

Key Points to Remember

- A value ladder moves people from free to paid—step by step.
- Your talk is the entry point, not the end.
- Every talk builds trust and creates opportunities for income.
- Conversations really do equal cash.

Mic Drop Moment

"A talk without a next step is just inspiration. A talk with a value ladder is a business."

Affirmation

"My message leads to transformation, my offers create impact, and my ladder turns inspiration into income."

Prompt for AI

Act as a business coach. Map out a value ladder for a speaker whose main topic is helping women build confidence in leadership roles.

Smart Thinking: Stretch your message across levels. Create a free offer, a mid-tier product, and a premium service. One message can lead to many streams when you think beyond the talk.

Implementation Assignment

Take your signature talk and map it into a simple value ladder:

- **Top rung:** Free lead magnet (guide, checklist, or resource).
- **Middle rung:** Paid workshop, group coaching, or mini-course.
- **Top rung:** Premium offer (signature program, VIP day, or corporate training).

Write it out and identify one step you can build this month.

Step Into the Spotlight Recap

Your talk is the door-opener, but your value ladder is what sustains your business. When you create a clear pathway from free to paid, you turn inspiration into transformation—and clients. Step into the spotlight by building a ladder that multiplies your message and your income.

Speaker's Get Paid Checklist

1. Create a lead magnet tied directly to your talk.
2. Design a landing page and QR code for easy sign-up.
3. Write a short email nurture sequence (3–5 emails).
4. Plan a free or low-cost workshop, webinar, or live session.

5. Develop a higher-ticket offer (coaching, training, or program).
6. Practice your closing so you confidently invite people to your freebie.
7. Include your lead magnet link on slides, handouts, and social media.
8. Schedule follow-up emails to invite people to your next offer.
9. Track how many people move from each ladder step to the next.
10. Refine your ladder after every event to improve results.

Trainings for you as you grow or scale your coaching and speaking business

Podia https://marshalynnhudson.podia.com/

Youtube https://www.youtube.com/@MarshaLynnHudson

Payhip https://payhip.com/marshalynnhudson

Newsletter https://marshalynnhudson.substack.com/

Marsha Hudson Media https://marshahudsonmedia.com/

Chapter 8

Grow Your Email List from Zero – Build Your Audience, Build Your Income

"If you're not showing up online, you're invisible to the people who need you."

Social media is great for visibility, but here's the truth—your followers don't belong to you. Algorithms change. Accounts get hacked. Platforms disappear. But your email list? That's yours. You control it, you own it, and it's the most direct line you'll ever have to the people who want to hear from you. If you're a speaker, your email list is your long-term profit plan. It's how you turn one-time event attendees into lifelong fans, clients, and customers.

One of the biggest mistakes speakers and coaches make is ignoring their email list. We get so caught up in social media that we forget the one thing we actually own—our list. Algorithms change. Platforms shift. But your email list? That's yours. It's your direct line to people who have already said "yes" to hearing from you. If you're starting with zero, that's okay. Every big list started with one subscriber. You can grow from there—strategically, simply, and steadily.

The key is offering value. Don't just say, "Join my list." That's not enough anymore. Give people a reason to exchange their email for something useful—like a checklist, guide, template, or training. These are called lead magnets, and they work. Think about what your audience needs right now. What's one quick win you could offer that relates to your message? Start there. Keep it simple and easy to deliver.

You can also grow your list through your speaking. Whether you're presenting in person or online, always mention your freebie. Say something like, "If you want a free resource to help you get started, head over to my website" or "Scan this QR code and grab my free workbook." This turns listeners into subscribers—right there in the moment while they're inspired. Don't overthink it—just include a strong call-to-action at the end of your talk. Make it feel like a bonus, not a sales pitch. People love free, helpful tools—especially when they're already feeling motivated.

Social media can also fuel your list. Every few posts, talk about your free resource. Create a pinned post or a link in bio with your lead magnet. Share behind-the-scenes of what they'll get. Use stories and short videos to invite them in. If you go live, drop the link in the comments. And don't forget to include it in your email signature, podcast outro, or anywhere your name shows up. You should always be leading people somewhere—and your list is the best place.

As your list grows, remember: it's not about numbers—it's about connection. Don't wait until you have 500 people to start writing to them. Start with 5. Show up with real stories, value, encouragement, and insight. Be consistent. Your list doesn't want perfection—they want authenticity and usefulness. If you serve them well, they'll stay—and some will eventually buy.

Another great way to grow your list is through collaborations. Partner with someone who has a similar audience and cross-promote each other's free offers. You can also speak at summits, guest on podcasts, or do joint workshops. Always bring a resource to share. These moments introduce you to new people—and the right ones will want to keep hearing from you. This is how you plant seeds for long-term growth.

You don't need tech overwhelm to start. Use a simple landing page builder like Mailer Lite, Kit.com, or Constant Contact. Set up an email welcome sequence with 3 to 5 messages. Thank them for subscribing, introduce who you are, and share your heart. It doesn't have to be perfect—it just has to be genuine. Keep everything aligned with your message and mission. Show people they're not just a name on a list—they're part of your community.

Your email list is where your message becomes a movement. It's how you nurture leads into clients, build trust at scale, and stay visible—no matter what happens to the algorithms. Don't wait until you feel "ready." Start now, start small, and stay consistent. One name turns into ten. Ten into a hundred. And before you know it, you have a powerful audience that shows up, shares your message, and supports your offers. Build it with heart—and it will grow with purpose.

Milestone Marker

By the end of this chapter, you should have:

- Created or chosen one lead magnet to attract subscribers.
- Set up a simple sign-up form or landing page to capture emails.
- Committed to consistently inviting people from talks, social posts, and conversations to join your list.

Why Email Beats Everything Else

You might be thinking, "Do people even open emails anymore?" The answer is yes—if your emails matter to them. Unlike social media, where you're fighting for attention in a noisy feed, email is personal. It lands directly in someone's inbox. It's intimate. And when done right, it builds trust faster than any platform out there. Your email list is also the heart of your **value ladder** (from Chapter 7). Without a list, your lead magnets, workshops, and offers don't have anywhere to go.

My Story: The Event That Changed How I See Email

Years ago, I spoke at a women's conference with 200 people in the room. My talk went great, but I didn't collect a single email. Two weeks later, I had no way to follow up. I had inspired a room full of potential clients—and then let them walk right out of my life. Fast forward to another event where I offered a free guide tied to my talk. I had a QR code on the screen, a sign-up sheet at the back, and my link printed on my handout. That day, 47 people joined my list. Within 30 days, 10 had purchased a low-ticket product, and two became coaching clients. That's the difference email makes.

Setting Up Your System for Getting Leads

A strong brand is great. A solid message is powerful. But without a system to bring in leads, you're just hoping to be found. If you want to grow your business, you need a **lead generation system**—one that runs in the background, brings new people into your world regularly, and helps you build relationships at scale.

Here's how to do it in a simple, sustainable way.

STEP 1: Create a Lead Magnet That Solves a Specific Problem

Your lead magnet should be short, actionable, and laser-focused. Think: checklist, cheat sheet, short training, or swipe file.
Key question: *What quick win can you give your audience in 10 minutes or less?*

Example: "5 Prompts to Craft a Signature Talk That Sells"
Example: "The Speaker Toolkit: Get Booked and Paid with Confidence"

STEP 2: Set Up a Landing Page + Email System

Use platforms like **Podia, Kit, or Constant Contact** to create:

- A branded landing page
- A thank you page with a follow-up offer or CTA
- A welcome email sequence (3–5 emails)

Pro Tip: Include a call to action in the first email (e.g., "Reply and tell me your biggest challenge" or "Here's how you can work with me").

STEP 3: Drive Traffic to Your Lead Magnet Weekly

You don't need to "go viral." You just need consistent visibility.
Here's how to drive weekly traffic to your lead magnet:

- Include the link in your Instagram bio, Facebook posts, and YouTube descriptions
- Mention it in every talk, podcast, or video
- Post 2–3 pieces of content per week that naturally lead into it
- Use DM scripts and "comment to get the freebie" posts to generate leads manually

STEP 4: Turn Leads into Conversations

Once someone joins your list or downloads your freebie, the goal isn't just to **collect**—it's to **connect**.

- Send personalized follow-ups when possible
- Offer free value like a podcast, training, or strategy call
- Ask questions, send check-in emails, and build the relationship

Remember: **People buy from people they trust**—and trust is built through consistent, caring touchpoints.

List-Building in the Room

As a speaker, you have a powerful advantage—you have a *live* audience already listening to you. Here's how to make the most of it:

1. **Offer Value, Not Just a Sign-Up** – Don't say, "Join my list." Say, "Grab my free guide to put today's talk into action."
2. **Make It Easy** – Use a QR code on your slides, a short link, and a sign-up sheet for those who prefer paper.
3. **Mention It More Than Once** – Bring it up early in your talk, in the middle, and again at the end.
4. **Give an Immediate Benefit** – If possible, have the freebie emailed instantly so they can see it before they leave the room.
5. **Include a Low-Cost Offer** – If you're ready, pair your freebie with a $17–$47 product to cover printing or travel costs

How to Start from Zero and Grow Quickly

- **Choose One Lead Magnet** – Create something irresistible for your audience.
- **Use Your Value Ladder** – Make sure your freebie is the first step toward your paid offers.
- **Promote It Everywhere** – Website, social media bios, speaking engagements, and even your email signature.
- **Nurture New Subscribers** – Don't just collect emails—build relationships. Send helpful tips, stories, and invitations to your offers.

Get Paid!

Your list is not just a group of names—it's your future revenue. When you launch a new workshop, book, or program, your list will be the first to hear about it. And because they've already connected with you, they're far more likely to buy. Even if you start with just 20 people, treat that list like gold. If each person on your list could become a $500 client or a $50 product buyer, you can see how quickly your list becomes a profit center.

Problem & Solution

Problem: Many speakers leave events with nothing but applause and no way to follow up with the audience. **Solution:** Use every speaking opportunity to grow your list, then nurture that list with value and offers.

Imagine this Scenario

She had no email list—just a message and a mission. Instead of waiting, she took action. She created a simple freebie from her talk, shared it at the end of her presentations, and promoted it consistently on social media. In a few short months, her list grew from zero to over 1,000 engaged subscribers. That list became her community, her test group, and eventually, her clients.

My Mindset Shift

I used to worry about views and likes. I'd post something, and if it didn't take off, I felt discouraged. But over time, I realized those numbers didn't matter as much as I thought. What really changed everything was my email list. The people who joined wanted to hear from me. They were more likely to open my emails, click on links, buy my products, and book my coaching. It wasn't about going viral. It was about building *value* and *connection*. **You don't need thousands. You need the right few who say yes.** And you build that, one person at a time.

Common Mistakes and How to Avoid Them

- **Mistake:** Relying only on social media followers.
  Avoid it: Build an email list you own—it's your direct connection to your audience.
- **Mistake:** Not giving people a reason to sign up.
  Avoid it: Offer a valuable, quick-win resource that solves a problem for them.
- **Mistake:** Overcomplicating the tech.
  Avoid it: Start with a simple email service and one landing page—then build later

Words of Wisdom

Your list is your legacy. Every name represents a person you can help, serve, and impact beyond the stage.

Step-by-Step Action Plan: Grow Your Email List from Zero

1. Create one lead magnet your audience will love.
2. Add it to every speaking presentation, handout, and bio link.
3. Use a QR code for quick sign-ups in the room.
4. Set up a welcome email to deliver the freebie instantly.
5. Commit to sending one valuable email per week.

Quick Wins

- Choose your lead magnet topic today.
- Sign up for an email marketing platform (ConvertKit, MailerLite, or Mailchimp).
- Create a landing page and connect it to your email platform.
- Announce your lead magnet on social media this week.

Journal Prompt

If my email list doubled or tripled in size over the next 90 days, how could that change my business?

_____

_____

_____

Reflection

My biggest takeaway:

_____

My next move:

_____

Key Points to Remember

- Your list is your most valuable asset.
- Live speaking events are prime opportunities to grow your list.
- A small, engaged list is better than a big, inactive one.
- Nurture your subscribers with value before you sell.

Mic Drop Moment

"The stage gives you visibility—your email list gives you longevity."

Affirmation

"My email list grows every week, and every name is a connection I value and nurture."

Prompt for AI

Act as a marketing strategist. Create a 4-week email nurture sequence for a speaker who teaches women how to turn their stories into income.

Smart Thinking: Likes are nice, but your list is your legacy. Treat every subscriber like a conversation waiting to happen. Serve them well, and they will show up for you.

Implementation Assignment

Choose one lead magnet idea and set up a sign-up form today. Share it once on social media or at the end of a presentation this week. Keep it simple—your goal is to start building, not to perfect the system.

Step Into the Spotlight Recap

An email list is your stage that never closes. When you grow it intentionally, you build relationships that last far beyond any event. Step into the spotlight by inviting people into your world where you can nurture, teach, and serve them consistently.

Speaker's Get Paid Checklist – For Growing Your Email List

1. Create a lead magnet tied directly to your talk's topic.
2. Add a QR code, link, and sign-up sheet to every speaking engagement.
3. Set up automated delivery of your freebie.
4. Write a welcome email that introduces you and your offers.
5. Send one value-packed email per week (tip, story, or resource).
6. Promote your lead magnet on at least two social media platforms.
7. Add your sign-up link to your website, bios, and email signature.
8. Track your growth monthly and set list-building goals.
9. Invite your list to a free or low-cost event regularly.
10. Use your list to launch offers, workshops, and products.

Chapter 9

Master the Discovery Call – Turning Conversations into Clients

"The goal isn't to sell on a discovery call—it's to connect, qualify, and invite."

A discovery call is one of the most powerful tools in your speaking business. It's where casual interest turns into committed action. It's also where a lot of speakers drop the ball—either by avoiding calls altogether because they don't want to feel "salesy" or by turning them into a hard pitch that leaves people feeling pressured.

The truth? When done right, a discovery call is simply a conversation. It's about understanding the person in front of you, learning what they need, and seeing if you're the right fit to help them. When you approach it that way, selling becomes serving.

Let's be real—discovery calls can feel intimidating when you're first starting out. You want to share your offer, but you don't want to sound pushy. You want to help, but you don't want to feel salesy. The good news is: a great discovery call doesn't feel like a sales pitch. It feels like a conversation. One person asking questions. Another person being heard. And both people exploring what's possible. That's it. Keep it human, not perfect.

Start by shifting your mindset. This call isn't about convincing—it's about connecting. You're not here to force someone into your program. You're here to see if your solution aligns with their struggle. That's it. Your energy should be calm, curious, and confident. You're offering guidance, not pressure. When you make it about service, the whole vibe changes—and people feel that.

Have a simple structure. First, thank them for their time and set the tone. Then ask about their goals, struggles, and what they've already tried. Listen deeply. Take notes. Don't rush. When they're done, repeat back what you heard to show you understand. Then ask if they'd like you to share how you might be able to help. This gives them the power to say yes.

When it's your turn to speak, be clear and kind. Share how your service or program can support their goal. Explain the transformation, not just the features. Tell a quick story about a client you helped—or your own experience. Paint the picture of what life could look like after working with you. Then share the details: how long, what's included, the investment. Pause. Ask if they have questions. Let them talk.

If they hesitate, don't panic. Objections are normal—it means they're thinking. Ask gentle questions: "What's holding you back?" or "What would make this feel like a yes for you?" Sometimes it's timing. Sometimes it's fear. Sometimes they just need reassurance. Don't try to "handle" their objection like a script—just keep the conversation open and honest. And whatever they decide, respect it.

Whether they say yes or no, follow up. Thank them for their time. If they weren't ready, offer a free resource or invite them to stay on your list. You never know when someone will circle back. I've had people say no—and sign up six months later. The seed you plant today may bloom later. Keep nurturing your people. It's never wasted.

Your confidence will grow with each call. Record your early ones (with permission), reflect on what went well, and improve your flow. You'll start to recognize patterns—what questions to ask, how to respond, and when to close the call with ease. The goal isn't to be perfect—it's to be prepared, personal, and professional. When people feel seen and heard, they trust you. And trust leads to conversion.

The discovery call is where your passion meets their pain point. It's not about fancy scripts—it's about sincere connection. You don't need to chase clients. You need to invite the right ones in and let your offer be the bridge. So take a deep breath, show up fully, and trust the process. The more you practice, the more natural it becomes. And soon, these calls will become one of your favorite parts of the business.

Every discovery call is also a discovery for you. You learn more about your audience—what they're struggling with, what they're dreaming about, and how they talk about their pain. These insights are golden. You can use them to improve your offers, your content, and even your messaging. I've updated my own programs simply from what people shared on calls. So instead of seeing these calls as just a "yes or no," see them as research. Every "no" is data. Every "yes" is confirmation. Either way—you win.

Don't be afraid to show your personality. I laugh with people on my calls. I share my story. I tell them I've been where they are. Because I have. People don't want a robot—they want a real person with real results. They want to feel safe. And when they feel that with you, they'll want to work with you. Let your light come through. This is your brand. Your voice. Your story.

And remember, you are the guide—not the hero. Your job is to help them see that a better outcome is possible. You're not trying to save them; you're helping them save themselves. This shift is powerful. It keeps you in service, not in stress. The discovery call is your moment to stand firm in your value, listen with love, and make a clear invitation. It's not about pressure—it's about partnership.

Milestone Marker

By the end of this chapter, you should have:

- A simple flow for your discovery calls (connect, explore, share, invite).
- A set of 5–7 open-ended questions to uncover client needs.
- The confidence to guide a call without feeling salesy.

Why Discovery Calls Matter for Speakers

Your talk creates curiosity. Your lead magnet builds trust. Your email nurture sequence builds connection. But the discovery call is where you find out if someone is ready to work with you—and if you can help them get the results they want. Without this step, you're leaving money on the table. People often need that one-on-one touch to make the decision to hire you, join your program, or book you for a workshop. Think about it—if someone has heard you speak, resonated with your message, and then takes the time to book a call, they are already interested. Your job isn't to "convince" them—it's to help them see whether working together makes sense for both of you.

My Story: From "Awkward" to Confident Closer

When I started doing discovery calls, I made every mistake in the book. I talked too much about myself. I gave away a full coaching session for free. I asked, "So... do you want to work together?" in a shaky voice at the end.

Then I shifted my mindset. I stopped thinking of them as sales calls and started treating them as clarity sessions for the other person. I asked better questions, listened more than I spoke, and invited them to take the next step if it made sense. My close rate shot up—not because I learned a magic script, but because I learned to lead with curiosity and confidence.

The Discovery Call Flow

Here's the simple flow I use and teach my clients:

1. **Welcome & Connection (2–3 min)** – Break the ice, thank them for their time, and make them feel comfortable.
2. **Explore Their Situation (5–10 min)** – Ask open-ended questions about their challenges, goals, and what's holding them back.
3. **Share Your Insights (3–5 min)** – Reflect back what you've heard and offer a perspective or a tip that shows you understand their situation.
4. **Present the Next Step (3–5 min)** – If it's a good fit, explain how you can help and outline the offer.
5. **Invite a Decision (2–3 min)** – Ask, "Would you like to move forward?" and let them answer without rushing.

Building Connection Before the Call

A discovery call doesn't start when you say "hello." It starts the moment someone books it. The confirmation email you send, the welcome video you share, or the prep questions you include all help set the tone. I like to send a short, friendly video thanking them for booking the call and letting them know what to expect. This lowers anxiety and makes the conversation feel warmer from the start.

Asking the Right Questions

The best calls are 70% them talking and 30% you talking. That means you need strong questions that draw out their real needs and goals. Instead of "What are you looking for?" ask:

- "What's the biggest challenge you're facing right now?"
- "What would change for you if this challenge was solved?"
- "Why is this the right time for you to make a change?"

These questions don't just give you information—they help the other person articulate the value of taking action.

Painting the Vision of What's Possible

One of the most powerful things you can do on a discovery call is to help the other person see what's possible for them. After listening to their challenges, describe a vision of the future they could step into if they solved the problem they've shared. This isn't about making unrealistic promises—it's about helping them see the potential and creating hope. People take action when they believe a better outcome is possible.

Handling Objections Without Pressure

Even when someone is a great fit, they might hesitate because of budget, timing, or fear. Instead of getting defensive, I acknowledge the concern and bring the focus back to their goals.

For example:
"I understand this is a big investment. The real question is—do you believe this will help you get where you want to go faster?" By keeping the conversation focused on results, you help them make a decision that feels right for them.

Showing Up as the Guide, Not the Hero

A mistake many speakers make on discovery calls is trying to "impress" the prospect by talking about themselves the entire time. Your role isn't to be the hero—it's to be the guide. The hero of the conversation is the person you're speaking to. Your job is to help them see that you have the tools, framework, and support to help them reach their own goals.

Follow-Up Is Where the Money Is

Not every call will end with a "yes" on the spot—and that's okay. But never let the conversation die there. Send a follow-up email within 24 hours recapping the call, restating the offer, and inviting them to reach out with questions. I've had people come back weeks or even months later and say, "I'm ready now." If you disappear after the first "no," you'll never give them the chance to circle back.

Leverage Every Call for Growth

Even if a call doesn't result in a sale, it's still valuable. Each conversation is an opportunity to refine your questions, improve your delivery, and learn more about your ideal clients. I keep a call journal where I jot down what worked, what didn't, and what I might try next time. Over time, this has made me sharper, more confident, and more effective.

Practice Makes Confident

Like speaking, discovery calls get easier the more you do them. If you're nervous, start by offering calls to warm leads—people already in your network, past clients, or those who've attended your events. Record your calls (with permission) and listen back. Notice your tone, pacing, and where you could have asked a better question. Small tweaks add up to big improvements in your close rate.

Conversations = Cash

Remember the value ladder from Chapter 7? The discovery call is often the final rung before a new client steps into your higher-ticket offer. It's where casual interest becomes commitment. And here's the thing—you don't need hundreds of calls to hit your goals. A handful of intentional, qualified calls each month can fill your calendar, your programs, and your bank account.

Get Paid!

When you master discovery calls, you shorten your sales cycle. Instead of waiting for people to "think about it" for months, you give them clarity and an opportunity to act now. And because you're speaking to people who have already experienced your talk, your content, or your lead magnet, they're warmer leads—which means higher conversion rates and less effort to close.

Problem & Solution

Problem: Many speakers inspire interest but never take the next step to have a real conversation that leads to a booking or sale.
Solution: Use a simple, service-based discovery call process to connect, qualify, and invite people into your offers.

Imagine this Scenario

She used to dread sales calls—rambling through them, unsure how to close without feeling salesy. But once she learned how to lead a discovery call with confidence, everything changed. She created a simple script based on her talk, asked powerful questions, and focused on the transformation her offer provided. The result? Her calls felt like coaching, not selling—and her conversion rate soared. What used to feel awkward became her favorite part of business: connecting and enrolling with ease.

My Mindset Shift

I used to dread discovery calls. I felt like I had to "sell" myself. I worried about sounding too pushy or saying the wrong thing. But then I shifted my mindset. I stopped treating it like a pitch—and started treating it like a conversation. I realized: this isn't about convincing anyone. It's about *clarity*. It's about helping someone see what's possible and how I can support them—if it's the right fit. Once I let go of the pressure to close, I showed up more confident, more connected, and more authentic.

And guess what?
More people said yes. Because they felt seen. Heard. Understood.

People aren't looking for a perfect pitch. They're looking for a person they can trust.

Common Mistakes and How to Avoid Them

- **Mistake:** Treating the call like a full free coaching session.
  Avoid it: Share insights, but save your full solutions for paying clients.
- **Mistake:** Talking too much about yourself.
  Avoid it: Let them do 70% of the talking while you guide the conversation.
- **Mistake:** Ending without a clear next step.
  Avoid it: Always close by inviting them to your offer if it's a good fit.

Words of Wisdom

The right conversation with the right person at the right time can change everything—for them and for you.

Step-by-Step Action Plan: Master Your Discovery Call

1. Decide on your call length (15–30 minutes works best).
2. Create 5–7 open-ended questions to uncover their needs.
3. Practice your call flow until it feels natural.
4. Have a clear next step to invite them into.
5. Block weekly time on your calendar for calls.

Quick Wins

- Add a "Book a Call" link to your emails, website, and social media.
- Practice your welcome and closing so you sound confident.
- Role-play a discovery call with a friend or colleague.
- Review your last 3 calls and note where you could improve.

Journal Prompt

If I booked 5 discovery calls a week, how could that change my income and impact?

_____

_____

_____

Reflection

My biggest takeaway:

_____

My next move:

_____

Key Points to Remember

- Discovery calls are about connection, not pressure.
- The goal is clarity—both for you and the other person.
- Conversations are often the fastest path to cash.
- A simple process beats a complicated script every time.

Mic Drop Moment

"When you stop trying to sell and start trying to serve, the right people will say yes."

Affirmation

"I lead discovery calls with confidence, clarity, and care—and the right clients say yes."

Prompt for AI

Act as a sales coach. Create a 7-question discovery call script for a speaker who helps women leaders grow their influence and income.

Smart Thinking: *Reframe the call. It's not about "closing"—it's about inviting someone into transformation. Ask more, listen deeply, and offer a solution that change*

Implementation Assignment

Write out your discovery call flow in 5 steps. Role-play it with a trusted friend or colleague this week. Practice closing with confidence by saying, "Would you like to move forward?" and sitting in the silence while they respond.

Step Into the Spotlight Recap

Discovery calls are not about pushing—they're about connecting. When you lead with clarity and care, you make it easy for the right clients to say yes. Step into the spotlight by mastering conversations that transform into opportunities.

Speaker's Get Paid Checklist

1. Decide on your ideal call length and purpose.
2. Create 5–7 open-ended questions for the call.
3. Practice your call flow until you can lead it without notes.
4. Have a clear, concise way to present your offer.
5. Add your "Book a Call" link to your emails, website, and presentations.
6. Invite people from your webinars, workshops, and events to book a call.
7. Block time on your calendar each week for discovery calls.
8. Track your close rate and work to improve it over time.

9. Follow up with every call, even if the person isn't ready to buy.
10. Celebrate each yes—and learn from each no.

Trainings for you as you grow or scale your coaching and speaking business

Podia https://marshalynnhudson.podia.com/

Youtube https://www.youtube.com/@MarshaLynnHudson

Payhip https://payhip.com/marshalynnhudson

Newsletter https://marshalynnhudson.substack.com/

Marsha Hudson Media https://marshahudsonmedia.com/

Chapter 10

Keep Learning, Keep Earning – Staying Relevant, Profitable, and In Demand

"Your growth is the foundation of your next opportunity."

In this industry, your skills, message, and business can only grow as far as you do. The most in-demand speakers and coaches are the ones who stay sharp, adaptable, and committed to personal and professional development. Yet too many people hit a plateau—they get comfortable with their talk, their slides, and their usual process. And then they wonder why bookings slow down or their business stops growing. The truth? You can't keep earning if you stop learning.

When I first stepped into this world of speaking, coaching, and online business, I thought learning ended once I launched. But I quickly realized the more I invested in learning, the more I grew—and the more I earned. Every workshop I attended, every book I read, every mentor I hired—it all sharpened my voice and clarified my message. I became more confident, more creative, and more effective. You don't need to know everything at once, but you do need to stay teachable. That's how you stay relevant in a changing world. When you keep learning, your audience keeps leaning in.

Success doesn't come from doing more—it comes from growing deeper. And personal growth fuels professional growth. When I work on my mindset, my money grows.

When I strengthen my routines, my results follow. You have to be willing to reflect, refine, and reset. The version of you that got you here won't get you there. If you want to reach new levels, you have to upgrade your habits, your environment, and sometimes even your circle.

Learning doesn't always look like taking a course. Sometimes it looks like slowing down to process what's working and what's not. Sometimes it's practicing your pitch until it sounds like poetry. Sometimes it's watching your favorite speakers and noting how they open and close their talks. You can learn from podcasts, YouTube videos, books, and even your own past mistakes. Growth doesn't have to be expensive, but it must be intentional. Learning is your secret weapon—don't leave it on the shelf.

One of the best decisions I made was joining communities of other women in business. When you're surrounded by people who are growing, it challenges you to stretch. It's easy to shrink when you're the smartest one in the room. But when you step into rooms where people are doing what you want to do, your vision expands. Collaboration replaces comparison. Instead of feeling behind, you start to feel inspired. Growth loves company.

The truth is: what got you booked once won't get you booked again and again. Audiences change. Platforms change. Messaging evolves. That's why you must evolve, too. Staying stuck in old strategies is a sure way to get left behind. But when you stay curious and open, you stay magnetic. The more you grow, the more your brand expands—and the more opportunities come your way.

As you keep learning, you build a library of value within yourself. This is where your signature stories, frameworks, and teachings are born. Every lesson you master becomes something you can teach. And that's the beauty of this journey—you're not just learning for yourself, you're learning for the people you're called to serve. The more you grow, the more you have to give. You are your best investment. Don't forget that.

There was a time when I thought I needed to be perfect before I could teach. But I learned that people connect more with your journey than your arrival. You can lead from the middle. You can teach what you just overcame. Your voice has value even if you're still learning. Don't wait until you "have it all together." Share what you're learning now—it could be the breakthrough someone else needs today.

So here's my challenge to you: never stop being a student. Make growth part of your brand. Read, ask questions, try new things, and don't be afraid to be a beginner again. Beginners have the most courage. They're not afraid to look foolish for the sake of becoming better. And better is where your next level lives.

Milestone Marker

By the end of this chapter, you should have:

- Identified one new skill or area of growth to focus on this quarter.
- Scheduled regular time for learning (reading, courses, or mentorship).
- A plan to apply what you learn directly to your speaking or business.

Why Continued Learning Matters for Speakers

The speaking industry is always evolving. Event formats shift. Technology changes the way audiences consume information. New social media platforms rise while others fade. Companies are looking for speakers who can address current issues, bring fresh perspectives, and adapt to different settings—whether that's a live stage, a virtual event, or a hybrid conference. When you commit to learning, you stay relevant and valuable.

Every new skill you gain becomes an asset you can monetize. Maybe you learn how to deliver high-energy virtual presentations. Maybe you master short-form video content that grows your audience. Or maybe you study sales psychology so you can close more coaching clients. Each time you expand your knowledge, you create new ways to serve and earn.

My Story: Growth That Paid Off

When I first started, my talk was my talk. I delivered it the same way every time. But I noticed other speakers getting invited back to the same events, while I wasn't. The difference? They kept evolving. They brought new stories, fresh strategies, and up-to-date insights. I decided to invest in a storytelling workshop and a high-level business mastermind. Within a year, I had doubled my speaking fee, added a signature workshop to my offerings, and was being referred for opportunities I would've never been considered for before. Growth wasn't just a nice idea—it was the reason my income jumped.

Learn Beyond the Stage

If you only study speaking, you'll only grow as a speaker. But your career is bigger than just the stage—it's a business. Learn marketing so you can promote yourself. Learn sales so you can confidently enroll clients. Learn leadership so you can inspire and manage a team as your business grows. The broader your skill set, the more opportunities you can say yes to—and get paid for.

Implement As You Learn

The biggest mistake I see is people who love to learn but never apply it. They collect notebooks full of ideas, but their presentations, offers, and strategies never change. Every time you learn something new, look for one way to implement it right away. Update a story in your talk. Try a new engagement technique. Launch a small program based on what you just learned. Action turns information into income. The landscape is shifting faster than ever. AI tools, hybrid events, micro-learning formats, and even audience attention spans are evolving. You don't have to master every new trend, but you do need to be aware of what's changing. That awareness lets you adapt before you're forced to, keeping you ahead of the competition instead of scrambling to catch up.

Build a Growth Network

Some of my best learning has come from conversations, not classrooms. Build relationships with other speakers, coaches, and industry leaders who share ideas, resources, and feedback. Attend masterminds, join professional associations, and be active in communities where people are moving forward. You'll pick up strategies that aren't in any book—and you'll make connections that lead to real opportunities. One of the fastest ways to cement your own learning is to teach it. Share a new insight with your audience in an email, on a livestream, or in a workshop. Not only will it reinforce the concept for you, but it also positions you as someone who is actively growing and bringing fresh value. Clients and event planners love that

Get Paid!

When you keep learning, you don't just stay relevant—you create leverage. You can increase your speaking fees because you're delivering more value. You can package new skills into workshops, courses, and programs. You can pivot into new markets and offer fresh solutions. Learning is not just about personal growth—it's about staying profitable in a competitive industry.

Problem & Solution

Problem: Many speakers stop growing once they feel "comfortable," and their opportunities dry up because they're not bringing anything new to the table.
Solution: Commit to continual learning in both your craft and your business so you remain relevant, valuable, and in demand.

Imagine this Scenario

She hit a plateau—her talks were good, but bookings stalled. Instead of quitting, she decided to invest in learning. She took one workshop on AI tools, another on storytelling for business, and listened to podcasts daily. Those small steps sparked big results. She updated her talk, automated her lead generation, and refined her signature program. Within months, new speaking invites came in, and she created a digital course that sold on autopilot. Her willingness to grow opened new doors—and turned her expertise into multiple income streams.

My Mindset Shift

There was a time when I thought I had to have it *all figured out* before I could be seen as a leader. But the truth is— growth doesn't stop once you launch your business or step on the stage. That's just the beginning. When I embraced a learner's mindset, everything shifted. I started investing in courses, coaches, and communities. Not because I was behind, but because I wanted to *stay ahead.* I learned to ask better questions. I learned how to refine my message. I learned how to *elevate* my value. Every new skill I picked up opened another door—whether it was a speaking opportunity, a client, or a new digital product I could sell. *The best investment you can make isn't in fancy tools—it's in your own growth.*

Common Mistakes and How to Avoid Them

- **Mistake:** Delivering the same talk year after year without refreshing.
  Avoid it: Update your stories, insights, and strategies regularly.
- **Mistake:** Collecting information but never applying it.
  Avoid it: Implement one action for every new lesson you learn.
- **Mistake:** Thinking you've "arrived" and don't need to keep growing.
  Avoid it: Stay curious—growth is what keeps you in demand.

Words of Wisdom

The stage will always welcome a woman who's prepared, relevant, and committed to her craft. Growth keeps you prepared.

Step-by-Step Action Plan: Keep Learning, Keep Earning

1. Choose one new skill to learn every quarter.
2. Schedule learning time into your calendar like you would a client call.
3. Find a mentor, mastermind, or peer group to accelerate your growth.
4. Apply each new concept within 30 days of learning it.
5. Track your wins to see how learning impacts your business.

Quick Wins

- Read one new book this month related to your craft or business.
- Follow three industry leaders and study their approach.
- Take a free online class in an area outside your comfort zone.
- Attend one networking event or workshop in the next 30 days.

Journal Prompt

What's one skill that, if I learned it in the next 90 days, would open new opportunities for me?

_____
_____
_____

Reflection

My biggest takeaway:

_____

My next move:

_____

Key Points to Remember

- Growth is the price of staying relevant.
- Every new skill can be turned into income.
- Learning beyond speaking expands your opportunities.
- Implementation is what turns knowledge into results.

Mic Drop Moment

"Your next level of income is hiding in your next lesson."

Affirmation

"I am committed to growth in my craft, my business, and my life. My learning keeps me relevant, in demand, and well-paid."

Prompt for AI

Act as a business growth coach. Create a 90-day learning and implementation plan for a professional speaker who wants to increase her fees and expand her offers.

Smart Thinking: The more you learn, the more you can teach. Every book, class, and room you step into expands what you can offer. Be a student of the journey.

Implementation Assignment

Choose one new book, online course, or mentor to learn from this month. Block out one hour a week on your calendar for growth. After each learning session, write down one action you'll take immediately.

Step Into the Spotlight Recap

Your growth is your greatest asset. The more you invest in learning, the more valuable you become to audiences, clients, and event organizers. Step into the spotlight by committing to growth that keeps you relevant, profitable, and in demand.

Speaker's Get Paid Checklist

1. Set a quarterly learning goal.
2. Allocate budget for personal and professional development.
3. Join at least one professional network or mastermind.
4. Attend one event—online or in person—every quarter.
5. Implement at least one new idea or strategy each month.
6. Share what you learn with your audience to increase authority.
7. Track how each learning investment impacts your income.
8. Evaluate and update your talk annually with new stories and insights.
9. Learn skills beyond speaking—marketing, sales, leadership.
10. Celebrate each growth milestone, no matter how small.

Chapter 11

Speaker Toolkit: Get Booked with Ease

"The easier you make it to say yes, the more often you'll hear it."

The secret to getting booked consistently as a speaker isn't just about being good on stage—it's about being easy to find, easy to understand, and easy to hire. That's what your speaker toolkit is for. It's the collection of materials that showcases your message, your professionalism, and your value. Event planners don't have time to chase down info or guess if you're a good fit. They want to see your expertise, your vibe, and your outcomes—all at a glance. A complete speaker toolkit makes that happen. If you want more yeses, make the decision effortless.

Your speaker toolkit isn't just a pretty package—it's your professional handshake. When someone opens your media kit or watches your speaker reel, they should instantly get a sense of who you are, what you stand for, and how you can transform a room. Make it clear, concise, and compelling. Include a strong bio, headshot, topics you speak on, testimonials, and a link to a short clip of you in action. Think of it as a mini stage—show up powerfully, even on paper.

A great speaker reel doesn't have to be fancy, but it does have to be real. Record a 60–90 second video introducing yourself, sharing a key point from one of your talks, and inviting people to book you. This is your chance to show your energy, expertise, and engagement skills. You don't need a full production crew—just your phone, a ring light, and a clear message. Speak from the heart. Speak with confidence. Speak to the person who is looking for someone just like you.

Don't wait to be discovered—be discoverable. That means having a speaker page on your website, a downloadable media kit, and links that work. Keep your content updated and your message focused. Decision-makers want to see that you're serious about your message and ready to go. When you make it easy for people to say yes to you, more people will. Make booking you a no-brainer.

Milestone Marker

By the end of this chapter, you should have:

- A simple **speaker toolkit** that includes a bio, headshot, and talk titles.
- Drafted or updated your **speaker one-sheet** or media kit.
- Identified one clip or recording you can use as part of your speaker reel.

Why a Speaker Toolkit Matters (find a sample on the resource page link)

Your talk opens the door, but your toolkit seals the deal. Event planners, conference organizers, and even podcast hosts are busy. They want to know what you speak about, who it helps, and why it matters. Your toolkit answers those questions before they even ask. A strong speaker toolkit builds trust, demonstrates professionalism, and shows you're ready. Without it, you blend in with the crowd. With it, you stand out.

Your toolkit also saves you time. Instead of writing a custom email every time someone asks for your info, you can send your one-sheet, link to your speaker page, and a short reel. It's efficient—and it positions you as someone who takes your message seriously.

My Story: Booked Because I Was Ready

Years ago, I applied to speak at a women's leadership summit. I didn't have the biggest following, but I had a clean one-sheet, a solid signature talk description, and a short video clip. The event host later told me, "We chose you because you made it easy for us to say yes." That taught me something I'll never forget: being prepared can be just as powerful as being popular. Since then, I've invested in updating my speaker page, refining my bio, and keeping my materials ready to send. And it's opened doors I never expected.

The Essential Elements

Speaker One-Sheet: A one-page PDF with your bio, talk titles, audience transformation, testimonials, and contact info. Think of it as your speaking resume.

Speaker Reel: A 2-3 minute video that shows you speaking and includes clips, testimonials, or audience engagement. If you're just starting out, film a simple demo of you delivering your message.

Professional Bio: Write a short (2-3 sentence) and long (1 paragraph) version. Include credibility, personality, and results.

Signature Talks: List 2-3 clear titles with bullet-point takeaways and outcomes. Speak to transformation, not just information.

Photos: High-quality headshots and lifestyle photos that match your brand. Organizers use these for promotion.

Website or Speaker Page: A simple page that includes your reel, talks, bio, photos, testimonials, and a contact form.

Testimonials: Social proof builds trust. Ask past clients or event hosts to provide short quotes about your impact.

Get Paid!

A polished toolkit positions you as a premium speaker. When your materials show you're organized, clear, and compelling, you can confidently charge higher fees. It also helps you get referred—because other people can send your one-sheet or link on your behalf. The more you streamline the process, the easier it becomes to scale. You're not just building a brand—you're building a business. And a strong toolkit is one of your best business assets.

Problem & Solution

Many speakers lose opportunities because they aren't prepared to promote themselves professionally. Solution: Create a complete, polished speaker toolkit that makes it easy for decision-makers to say yes.

Imagine this Scenario

She had the experience, the message, and the passion—but she wasn't getting booked. Then she created a simple speaker toolkit: a one-sheet, a short reel, a clear bio, and a pitch email. Nothing fancy—just strategic and aligned. In two weeks, she sent 10 pitches. Five responded. Three booked her. Having the right tools made her look professional and feel confident. It shifted the way others saw her—and how she saw herself. The toolkit didn't just open doors. It made her ready to walk through them.

My Mindset Shift

For a long time, I said I wanted more speaking engagements—but I didn't have anything ready to *send* when someone showed interest. No speaker one sheet. No updated bio. No professional photos. No reel. I wasn't ready for the *yes* I said I wanted. Everything changed when I started treating my speaking like a business, not a side hobby. I built my toolkit. I created a clear speaker page. I gathered testimonials and crafted a compelling signature talk. And here's what I realized: Opportunities flow more freely when you're prepared to receive them.

Common Mistakes and How to Avoid Them

- **Mistake:** Waiting until someone asks for materials to start creating them.
  Avoid it: Be prepared so you can send your toolkit instantly when an opportunity arises.
- **Mistake:** Overloading your kit with too much information.
  Avoid it: Keep it concise—highlight your message, transformation, and booking details.
- **Mistake:** Using outdated or poor-quality photos.
  Avoid it: Invest in a professional headshot that reflects your brand.

Words of Wisdom

Don't wait until someone asks—build your toolkit now, so when opportunity knocks, you're ready to walk through the door.

Step-by-Step Action Plan: Build Your Speaker Toolkit

Write your short and long bio. Create your speaker one-sheet with talk titles, outcomes, and testimonials. Film a 1-2 minute video showcasing your energy and message. Design a simple speaker page on your website. Write an email pitch you can copy and paste.

Quick Wins

Update your headshot. Ask a past client for a testimonial. Make a list of your top 3 talk titles and outcomes. Review and polish your speaker one-sheet.

Journal Prompt

What would a meeting planner think about me if they looked me up today?

_____
_____
_____

Reflection

My biggest takeaway:

_____

My next move:

_____

Key Points to Remember

- A speaker toolkit helps you stand out.
- Professionalism builds trust before you speak. Make it easy for people to say yes.
- Every yes begins with being prepared.

Mic Drop Moment

"Be ready so you don't have to get ready."

Affirmation

"I am a professional speaker, prepared and positioned to get booked with ease."

Prompt for AI

Act as a brand strategist. Create a speaker one-sheet template that includes bio, talk titles, takeaways, testimonials, and contact info.

Smart Thinking: The more you learn, the more you can teach. Every book, class, and room you step into expands what you can offer. Be a student of the journey—and watch your business evolve.

Implementation Assignment

Create or update your speaker one-sheet this week. Include your bio, signature talk titles, transformation statement, headshot, and contact information. Save it as a PDF so you can quickly send it to potential clients and event planners.

Step Into the Spotlight Recap

Your speaker toolkit is your credibility on paper. It shows decision-makers that you're not only inspiring on stage but also prepared and professional. Step into the spotlight by building a toolkit that makes getting booked easier than ever.

Speaker's Get Paid Checklist

- For Your Toolkit Write a professional bio (short + long version).
- Create a speaker one-sheet with titles, outcomes, testimonials.
- Record or update your speaker reel.
- Design a speaker page on your website.
- Have an email pitch template ready to send.
- Collect and organize 3–5 testimonials.
- Keep all materials in a folder for easy access.
- Refresh your toolkit every 6 months.

Trainings for you as you grow or scale your coaching and speaking business

Podia https://marshalynnhudson.podia.com/

Youtube https://www.youtube.com/@MarshaLynnHudson

Payhip https://payhip.com/marshalynnhudson

Newsletter https://marshalynnhudson.substack.com/

Marsha Hudson Media https://marshahudsonmedia.com/

- For the free audio training to accompany this book- go to: https://marshalynnhudson.podia.com/

PART THREE: MONETIZE THE MESSAGE

12. Sell Your Talk as a Workshop or Training
Package your talk for schools, companies, and conferences.

13. Build Bundles, Partnerships & Corporate Offers
Turn your message into customized offers businesses will buy.

14. Expand Your Brand Beyond the Stage
Create digital products, courses, books, and group programs.

15. Women Who Rock: Leave Your Legacy Now
Step fully into your calling, grow your audience, and create your ripple effect.

- For the free audio training to accompany this book- go to: https://marshalynnhudson.podia.com/

Chapter 12

Sell as a Workshop or Training – Keep Building, Keep Thriving

"Success isn't built in one big leap—it's sustained in the small steps you take consistently."

You've built your platform, expanded your reach, and learned how to turn your message into income. But here's the truth: the work doesn't stop when you hit a goal. If you want to keep thriving as a speaker and businesswoman, you have to nurture your growth and protect your momentum. Sustaining progress is an intentional act—it doesn't happen by accident.

In the speaking world, momentum is everything. You can have an amazing season of bookings and client work, but if you stop showing up, learning, and innovating, you'll lose that momentum faster than you built it. The good news? Sustaining growth doesn't require giant leaps—it's about small, consistent actions that keep you relevant, valuable, and in demand.

You don't have to stop at just giving a speech—your talk can become a full-blown workshop, training, or even a curriculum. What you're already teaching in 20 or 30 minutes can be expanded into a 60-minute workshop or a 3-hour training. This is how you multiply your opportunities without starting from scratch. The key is knowing that your voice has value, and your message can be monetized over and over in different formats.

Start by identifying the transformation your talk offers. What problem are you solving? What skill are you teaching? What shift are you helping people make? Once you're clear on the outcome, you can turn your talk into a hands-on experience. Add exercises, worksheets, group discussions, or a simple framework so participants walk away not just inspired—but equipped.

Organizations love content that helps their teams grow. If your talk covers leadership, communication, productivity, mindset, diversity, or any topic that supports growth— there's a good chance companies, schools, and nonprofits will pay you to deliver it as a training. Think of your message as a tool they can use to meet their goals. All you have to do is package it clearly.

A workshop doesn't need to be perfect—it needs to be practical. You can take one idea from your signature talk and break it into three parts: what, why, and how. Then add a simple activity under each part. That becomes your 60-minute workshop. You don't need fancy slides or professional design. You need clarity, confidence, and content that makes people think, feel, and take action.

One of the best things you can do is turn your talk into a PDF workbook or training guide. This gives the event organizer more value and shows that you're prepared and professional. A guide also helps your audience retain your message and refer back to it later. It positions you not just as a speaker—but as a teacher and trainer with lasting impact.

Once you've got a workshop, you can offer it in person, online, or hybrid. You can host your own sessions or pitch them to organizations. You can charge per seat or offer a flat fee. The flexibility is powerful. Every time you deliver it, you're also improving it—so don't wait until it's perfect. Teach what you know, and tweak as you grow.

Selling your talk as a training allows you to create scalable income. You can license it to companies, offer it as a recurring workshop, or turn it into a course. This is how you stop trading time for one speaking gig and start building a system where your message works for you. One talk can turn into many opportunities with the right structure.

You already have what you need. Your story, your strategies, and your voice are the foundation. Now it's time to think bigger. You're not just a speaker—you're a solution provider. And when you start positioning your talk as a workshop or training, you unlock new income streams and new levels of influence.

The women who stay booked and profitable aren't just talented—they're intentional. They treat their business like a living thing that needs care, attention, and fresh input. Growth isn't just about chasing new opportunities; it's about strengthening what you've already built so it can keep producing results.

Here's the reality:

- Skills fade if you stop sharpening them.
- Relationships weaken if you stop tending to them.
- Opportunities dry up if you stop showing up.

Your job as a speaker is not just to "get there" but to *stay there*—and that takes focus.

Milestone Marker

By the end of this chapter, you should have:

- Outlined how your keynote can be expanded into a full workshop or training.
- Identified at least one organization, school, or company to pitch your training to.
- Created a draft description of your workshop with clear outcomes.

My Story: The Year I Almost Lost My Momentum

There was a year early in my career when I coasted. I'd had a great run of speaking engagements, so I thought I could take my foot off the gas. I stopped networking, stopped posting regularly, and didn't invest in learning anything new. By the next year, my bookings had slowed to a trickle. That was my wake-up call: in this business, you have to keep planting seeds, even when you're busy harvesting.

The 3 P's of Sustained Success

1. Prioritize: Keep your most important activities—like outreach, learning, and relationship-building—at the top of your to-do list.
2. Protect: Guard your time and energy so you can keep showing up at your best.
3. Progress: Always be improving—your talk, your delivery, your offers, and your systems.

Sample Speaker & Workshop Proposal

Use this as a template to pitch yourself with clarity, professionalism, and confidence.

Name: Marsha Lynn Hudson
Title: Brand & Marketing Strategist | AI Consultant | The Queen of Systems
Email: marsha@marshalynnhudson.com
Website: www.marshahudsonmedia.com
LinkedIn: linkedin.com/in/marshalynnhudson

Proposal Title:

The Success Trifecta: Brand. Market. Lead. The 3 Book Trilogy -Crushing Barriers. Unstoppable Woman. Women Who Rock the Stage- Women's Empowerment Trilogy
Workshop or Keynote Presentation

Overview:

This workshop is designed to empower women with a proven 3-part system to build a powerful personal brand, market with clarity, and generate consistent leads. Ideal for conferences, organizations, women's business networks, or corporate employee resource groups.

Participants will leave with a clear framework, actionable tools, and renewed confidence in their ability to grow visibility and profit from their voice and expertise.

Learning Objectives:

By the end of this session, attendees will:

- Identify their unique brand message and positioning
- Understand how to market their expertise using a simple content system
- Learn how to turn visibility into leads and paying opportunities
- Walk away with tools to simplify and systematize their outreach

Format Options:

- 60-minute Keynote
- 90-minute Virtual or In-Person Workshop
- Half-Day or Full-Day Training with Workbook + Templates

Bonus:

Every participant will receive a downloadable Success Trifecta Workbook, including templates, checklists, and AI-powered tools for content and visibility.

Investment:

Pricing ranges based on session length and customization:

- **Virtual Workshop:** $750 – $1500
- **In-Person Half-Day:** $2500 – $5000
- **Full-Day Training with Assets:** $7500+

Customized packages available. Includes prep session and post-event resource bundle.

How to Keep Your Growth Alive

Continue Learning: Read books, take courses, attend conferences, and stay current with trends in your niche.
Stay Connected: Keep building and nurturing your network—past clients, audience members, and peers.
Evaluate Regularly: Every quarter, review what's working, what's not, and what needs to be updated in your brand and business.
Create Consistent Touchpoints: Send emails, post on social, and keep sharing your expertise so people don't forget about you.

Get Paid!

When you nurture your growth, you position yourself for long-term success. You can raise your fees because you're consistently improving your skills and expanding your expertise. You can book more repeat clients because you've stayed in touch and delivered value even after the event. You can create additional revenue streams—like workshops, courses, or products—because you've built a loyal audience that trusts you. Sustained growth is what turns a one-time gig into a thriving career.

Think of it this way: would you hire the speaker who's actively learning, posting valuable content, and staying engaged with their audience—or the one who hasn't updated anything in a year? The choice is obvious.

Problem & Solution

Problem: Many speakers slow down after reaching a milestone, causing their momentum—and income—to drop.

Solution: Commit to consistent actions that nurture your growth, maintain your visibility, and keep your skills sharp.

Imagine this Scenario

She started with a free 20-minute talk at a local women's group. After the event, someone from the audience approached her—an HR manager at a small company. That single moment led her to package her message as a 90-minute workshop with a workbook and slides. A few weeks later, she delivered her first paid training—and they asked her back for a team retreat. What began as a small, unpaid opportunity turned into a repeat corporate contract. Once she learned to sell her talk as a solution, everything changed.

My Mindset Shift

For years, I saw myself as *just* a speaker. I'd show up, pour into the audience, and leave with nothing more than applause. But the moment I realized companies and schools don't pay for "talks"—they invest in *solutions*—everything shifted.

You're not selling a speech.
You're offering a transformation.
You're solving a problem they have.

When you shift from "I hope they book me" to "Here's how I can help your team grow," doors open. Budgets appear. Contracts get signed. The value was always in your message. Now, package it like the solution it is.

Common Mistakes and How to Avoid Them

- **Mistake:** Treating your keynote and workshop as the same thing.
  Avoid it: A keynote inspires, a workshop equips. Always add tools, interaction, and outcomes.
- **Mistake:** Using generic descriptions that don't address client needs.
  Avoid it: Frame your workshop around their problems and the transformation you provide.
- **Mistake:** Underpricing trainings compared to keynotes.
  Avoid it: Workshops are deeper, longer, and often worth more—price accordingly.

Words of Wisdom

The stage will always welcome a woman who stays prepared, relevant, and committed to her craft. Growth is the result of showing up even after the applause fades.

Step-by-Step Action Plan: Nurture Your Growth

1. Set aside one hour each week for learning and skill-building.
2. Reach out to two past clients or event organizers every month.
3. Audit your brand materials and online presence quarterly.
4. Block time on your calendar for consistent content creation.
5. Add one new offer, service, or resource each year.

Quick Wins

- Follow one new thought leader in your industry.
- Post one valuable insight or story this week.
- Read one chapter of a personal development book today.

Journal Prompt

What habits and actions will keep my growth alive for the next 12 months?

_____

_____

_____

Reflection

My biggest takeaway:

_____

My next move:

_____

Key Points to Remember

- Growth requires intentional maintenance.
- Small, consistent actions keep your momentum alive.
- Stay connected, stay visible, and keep learning.
- Sustained growth is the foundation for long-term income.

Mic Drop Moment

"Momentum is earned every day—keep showing up for the future you're building."

Affirmation

"I am committed to nurturing my growth and protecting my momentum. I show up consistently for the life and business I am creating."

Prompt for AI

Act as a business strategist. Create a 12-month growth maintenance plan for a professional speaker who wants to increase repeat bookings and expand her offers.

Smart Thinking: Package your talk as a solution, not just a speech. Schools, nonprofits, and businesses are looking for content that empowers their people. Lead with transformation and back it up with structure.

Implementation Assignment

Take your signature talk and expand it into a **workshop outline** with:

- An introduction and icebreaker.
- 3–4 teaching modules with interactive elements.
- A closing action plan participants can take with them.

Write a short description of this workshop and keep it ready to send to potential clients.

Step Into the Spotlight Recap

Selling your talk as a workshop or training multiplies your opportunities and income. It shows organizations you can do more than inspire—you can help transform. Step into the spotlight by packaging your message into formats companies and schools are eager to buy.

Speaker's Get Paid Checklist

- Schedule weekly time for learning and skill-building.
- Maintain consistent content across your platforms.
- Check in with past clients regularly.
- Update your speaker reel, photos, and bio at least once a year.
- Track your progress and celebrate wins.
- Add new offers to keep your brand fresh.
- Protect your energy and avoid burnout.
- Continue networking, both online and offline.
- Review and refine your systems quarterly.

Chapter 13

Build Bundles, Partnerships & Corporate Offers – Multiply Your Income and Impact

"When you package your brilliance, you multiply your impact and income."

You've built your talk, refined your delivery, and started booking speaking engagements — but if you want to take your business to the next level, you have to think beyond the stage. The real magic happens when you turn your message into multiple offers that keep generating income long after the applause fades. That's where bundles, partnerships, and corporate offers come in.

In the speaking world, too many talented women limit themselves to a one-and-done model: one talk, one check. But your talk can be the starting point for workshops, trainings, consulting packages, and digital programs. When you package your expertise strategically, you give clients more value, open doors to bigger contracts, and create consistent revenue streams.

You don't have to do it all alone. In fact, the fastest way to grow your income and impact is through strategic bundles, partnerships, and corporate packages. Think of it like building your own success lane—with collaborators, not competitors. When you combine your expertise with others who serve a similar audience, you create more value—and more opportunity.

Bundles are powerful because they give your audience more without overwhelming you. You can package your keynote with a workbook, a follow-up Q&A, or a digital product. You can create a speaker + workshop combo, or bundle your course with a group coaching call. When you build a bundle, you increase your price—and your perceived value—without doing a lot more work.

Partnerships allow you to go further, faster. You might team up with a coach, consultant, or educator who teaches something that complements your talk. Together, you can co-host trainings, offer retreats, or pitch group programs to schools and organizations. When you collaborate with the right people, you gain access to their audience—and they gain access to yours. It's a win-win.

Corporate offers are where your speaker brand gets seriously profitable. Businesses and nonprofits are looking for trainers, workshop leaders, and speakers who can help them improve communication, culture, leadership, or productivity. You already have a message—they need a solution. When you present your offer as something that solves a pain point for their team, you position yourself as a partner, not just a presenter.

You don't need to overcomplicate your corporate package. Offer a 60-minute workshop, a workbook, a follow-up Zoom Q&A, and access to a replay or resource guide. That's a solid $2,500–$5,000 package. If you add a mini-course, private coaching, or a team assessment, that number can double or triple. The key is to focus on outcomes: what are they walking away with?

Many women underestimate how valuable their content is to businesses. If your message can help teams perform better, think better, or work better—then companies will pay for that. They pay consultants, coaches, and trainers every day. It's time you positioned yourself as one. Build a pitch, create a package, and start showing up in rooms where decisions are made.

Don't be afraid to repurpose. You don't need new content for each offer. You can take your core message and remix it into different formats: keynotes, workshops, courses, VIP days, or coaching. This allows you to meet clients where they are and scale your brand without burning out. Your brilliance isn't in how much you do—it's in how well you package it.

You have a message that can move people—and move companies forward. By thinking beyond the stage, you create a speaker brand that's sustainable, scalable, and profitable. Build your bundle. Form your partnerships. Pitch your package. The opportunities are out there. And you're already equipped to take them.

Milestone Marker

By the end of this chapter, you should have:

- Created at least one **bundle** that combines your keynote with workshops, coaching, or digital tools.
- Identified 2–3 potential partners you could collaborate with for greater reach.
- Drafted a simple **corporate package** that highlights clear outcomes for organizations.

Why Packaging Your Expertise Matters

Bundles, partnerships, and corporate offers allow you to maximize the impact of your work without constantly reinventing the wheel. Instead of chasing single bookings, you build offers that can be sold over and over again. This approach not only increases your income but also deepens your relationship with clients, leading to repeat business and referrals.

Here's the reality:

- One talk can lead to months of training work.
- One partnership can open the door to entire new audiences.
- One corporate contract can out-earn a year's worth of single events.

When you stop thinking of yourself as "just a speaker" and start seeing yourself as a problem-solver, you unlock bigger opportunities.

My Story: The First Time I Bundled My Offers

Early in my career, I spoke at a conference and gave it my all. The audience loved it, but once I stepped off stage, that was it — no follow-up, no additional income. A year later, I pitched the same conference a "speaker package" — my keynote, plus a breakout session, plus a post-event virtual training. Not only did they pay me three times more, but they invited me back the next year to do it again. That was the moment I realized the power of packaging my expertise.

The 3 C's of High-Value Offers

1. **Clarity** – Be clear on the transformation you provide and who your ideal client is.
2. **Customization** – Tailor your packages to meet specific audience or organizational needs.
3. **Consistency** – Deliver a repeatable, high-quality experience every single time.

How to Build Bundles, Partnerships, and Corporate Offers

Bundles: Combine multiple services and resources into a single package. For example, pair your keynote with a workshop, a workbook, and a follow-up coaching call. This increases perceived value and makes it easier for clients to justify the investment.

Partnerships: Team up with other speakers, trainers, or organizations that serve your audience. Partnerships can give you access to new markets, increase your credibility, and lead to long-term collaborations.

Corporate Offers: Package your expertise into training programs, leadership development series, or professional development packages. Companies are willing to pay more for solutions that address their biggest challenges — employee engagement, productivity, and retention.

Get Paid!

When you bundle your services, form strategic partnerships, and offer corporate packages, you move from one-off payments to long-term contracts. This allows you to stabilize your income, increase your rates, and build a reputation as a high-value, results-driven professional. Decision-makers are far more likely to invest in a speaker who can provide ongoing solutions rather than a single presentation. Think of it this way: Would a company rather hire someone for one hour... or someone who can lead a six-month training initiative that transforms their team? Exactly.

Problem & Solution

Problem: Many speakers leave money on the table by only offering single talks instead of packaged solutions.
Solution: Create bundles, partnerships, and corporate offers that give clients more value and allow you to maximize each opportunity.

Imagine this Scenario

She had a powerful talk that resonated with entrepreneurs, but she wanted to reach organizations. Instead of starting from scratch, she bundled her keynote with a mini-course, a workbook, and a follow-up group session. She pitched this bundle as a custom team development package—and a small company said yes. That one partnership turned into more. She realized companies don't just want inspiration— they want tools, training, and transformation. By repackaging her talk into a corporate offer, she stepped into a new income stream and a new level of authority.

My Mindset Shift

For a long time, I thought offering low-cost coaching sessions or one-off classes was the only way to grow. But when I stepped back and looked at what companies *actually* invest in—training, team development, leadership, communication—it hit me: I had been sitting on a goldmine.

Your message doesn't have to be boxed into one-hour talks or $97 offers. When you think like a CEO, you start creating *solutions*—packages, partnerships, and programs that solve real problems for organizations, schools, and businesses. You move from side hustle thinking to *sustainable impact*. **You don't just speak—you structure. You don't just coach—you consult. You don't just share—you scale.**

Common Mistakes and How to Avoid Them

- **Mistake:** Offering one-off talks with no follow-up.
  Avoid it: Position yourself as a long-term solution with bundled or corporate options.
- **Mistake:** Pricing bundles too low.
  Avoid it: Remember—companies budget thousands for professional development. Price for value, not hours.
- **Mistake:** Creating offers that are too generic.
  Avoid it: Customize for the company's needs— tailored = booked.

Words of Wisdom

Your talk is the door-opener, but your packages are the long-term income builder. When you think bigger than the stage, you create a business that works for you all year long.

Step-by-Step Action Plan: Build Bundles, Partnerships & Corporate Offers

1. Identify the core transformation you provide.
2. Create one bundle that includes at least three different touchpoints.
3. List five potential partners and reach out to explore collaborations.
4. Design one corporate offer with clear outcomes and deliverables.
5. Price your packages based on value, not just time.

Quick Wins

- Review your current offers and see how you can bundle them.
- Reach out to one potential partner this week.
- Create a one-page outline of your corporate offer.
- Add package details to your website and speaker materials.

Journal Prompt

If I could design one dream package that would deliver maximum value to my clients and maximum income for me, what would it look like?

_____

_____

_____

Reflection

My biggest takeaway:

_____

My next move:

_____

Key Points to Remember

- One talk can lead to months of work if you package it right.
- Partnerships can accelerate your reach and credibility.
- Corporate clients pay more for comprehensive solutions.
- Bundles increase value and simplify the buying decision.

Mic Drop Moment

"Stop selling single talks. Start selling solutions."

Affirmation

"I am a solutions provider. I package my brilliance to create impact, value, and sustainable income."

Prompt for AI

Act as a business strategist. Design three speaker bundles that combine keynotes, workshops, and follow-up services for maximum client value.

Smart Thinking: Stop thinking like a speaker. Start thinking like a business. Bundling your talk with a workbook, follow-up training, or digital product creates irresistible value for organizations.

Implementation Assignment

Sketch out one **corporate package** today. Example:

- Keynote (60 min)
- 2-part workshop (virtual or in-person)
- Workbook or digital toolkit
- Follow-up Q&A session

Give it a name and a clear outcome, then add it to your speaker toolkit.

Step Into the Spotlight Recap

Bundles, partnerships, and corporate offers multiply your income and influence. They position you as more than a speaker—they make you a trusted partner in solving organizational problems. Step into the spotlight by packaging your message in ways companies can't resist.

Speaker's Get Paid Checklist – For Bundles, Partnerships & Corporate Offers

- Define the transformation you provide.
- Identify and reach out to potential partners.
- Develop a corporate package with clear outcomes.
- Price your packages based on value delivered.
- Add bundles and offers to your marketing materials.
- Share success stories from past clients.
- Follow up with clients to renew or expand contracts.
- Deliver consistently high-quality experiences.

Trainings for you as you grow or scale your coaching and speaking business

Podia https://marshalynnhudson.podia.com/

Youtube https://www.youtube.com/@MarshaLynnHudson

Payhip https://payhip.com/marshalynnhudson

Newsletter https://marshalynnhudson.substack.com/

Marsha Hudson Media https://marshahudsonmedia.com/

Chapter 14

Expand Your Brand Beyond the Stage – Turn Your Message into Products, Programs, and Passive Income

"Your voice is powerful on stage — but your impact multiplies when you take it beyond the microphone."

You've built your speaking career, booked engagements, and learned how to create high-value offers. But the true potential of your message isn't limited to the stage. The smartest speakers find ways to expand their brand into products, programs, and other income streams that continue to serve people long after the event is over. This is how you turn a speaking career into a full, thriving business.

In today's world, audiences don't just want inspiration — they want transformation. And transformation takes time. You can make a huge impact in a 60-minute keynote, but when you offer follow-up programs, self-paced courses, books, and group experiences, you extend that transformation far beyond the event itself. That's the real power of expanding your brand.

You were never meant to stay on just one stage. Your voice, your expertise, and your message can live far beyond the microphone. Expanding your brand beyond the stage means packaging your story, your system, and your strategies into assets that can work for you every day—

even when you're not speaking. This is how you create sustainability, freedom, and multiple streams of income.

One of the simplest ways to start is with a digital product. You already have the content. You've been teaching it, speaking it, and living it. Now it's time to package it. Whether it's an ebook, a workbook, a mini course, or a resource bundle, digital products allow you to earn while you sleep and give your audience immediate transformation. They're low-maintenance and high-impact when done right.

Courses are another powerful way to go deeper. When someone hears you speak and loves your message, they often want more. Your course becomes the next step. It could be self-paced or live, big or small. What matters most is clarity—what are they learning, and what will they walk away with? You don't need a perfect studio setup. You just need your voice, your system, and a plan.

Books help you build credibility and legacy. If you've ever dreamed of becoming an author, now is the time. Turn your keynote into a book. Expand your podcast into chapters. Use your blog posts or workshop notes to form a manuscript. Your book becomes your business card, your platform-builder, and a tool to reach people in rooms you haven't even entered yet.

Group programs and masterminds allow you to coach and teach at scale. You don't have to do one-on-one if you don't want to. You can gather like-minded women around your core message and guide them through transformation together. Whether it's four weeks or six months, your voice becomes the catalyst for change. You lead the room—and the ripple effect begins.

Another powerful option is licensing your material. Companies, schools, and organizations are always looking for training tools. You can license your course, curriculum, or signature talk as part of their employee development. This allows your message to multiply without you having to be in the room. It's a way to serve at scale and earn consistently.

As you expand your brand, stay rooted in your core message. Don't create random offers. Build a clear brand ecosystem. Your keynote leads to your book. Your book leads to your course. Your course leads to your group program or workshop. This is how you guide your audience through a journey—and build a business that grows with you.

Your message is too powerful to only live on a stage. Let it live in your products, your programs, your platforms, and your partnerships. Let it expand beyond what you can imagine. The more you share your voice in new ways, the more people you impact—and the more income and influence you create.

Milestone Marker

By the end of this chapter, you should have:

- Chosen one way to repurpose your message into a product, program, or digital offer.
- Drafted a simple outline for your first product (e.g., mini-course, workbook, or coaching group).
- Identified how this new offer ties back to your talk and expands your reach.

Why Expanding Your Brand Matters

When you only offer live speaking, you limit your reach to the people in the room. But when you create digital products, group programs, or membership communities, your message can travel anywhere — and keep generating revenue while you focus on other opportunities.

Here's the reality:

- A book can reach thousands you'll never meet in person.
- An online course can serve people in every time zone.
- A membership program can provide consistent monthly income.

By expanding beyond the stage, you stop trading only time for money and start building assets that work for you 24/7.

My Story: From One Stage to Many Streams

For years, I saw myself solely as a speaker. Then one day, an audience member asked, "How can I keep learning from you?" That question sparked the creation of my first group coaching program. It sold out in two weeks — and it opened my eyes to the fact that people wanted more than just my keynote. They wanted ongoing support, tools, and resources. Since then, I've created courses, workshops, and even branded merchandise that allow me to serve in new ways while growing my income.

The 3 E's of Expanding Beyond the Stage

1. **Extend** – Take the core message from your keynote and extend it into programs, courses, and resources.
2. **Engage** – Build ongoing relationships through memberships, communities, or coaching programs.
3. **Elevate** – Use products and programs to raise your brand's authority and visibility.

How to Expand Your Brand Beyond the Stage

Products: Books, journals, workbooks, toolkits, and merchandise that carry your message into people's daily lives.
Programs: Group coaching, masterminds, workshops, and retreats that allow you to go deeper with your audience.
Digital Offers: Online courses, recorded trainings, and memberships that give you scalable, passive income.

Get Paid!

When you expand your brand beyond the stage, you create income streams that keep working without you physically being there. This allows you to serve more people, reach new markets, and create financial stability. The more ways people can work with you, the more opportunities you create for impact — and the more confident you can be in charging premium fees for your speaking. Think of it like this: an event organizer who knows you have follow-up programs is more likely to book you, because they see you as a partner in creating lasting change — not just a one-time speaker.

Problem & Solution

Problem: Relying solely on live speaking limits your reach, income, and long-term impact.
Solution: Create products, programs, and digital offers that expand your brand and serve your audience in multiple ways.

Imagine this Scenario

After years of speaking on stages, she realized she was leaving money on the table. She took her most requested talk and turned it into a digital course. Then she created a companion ebook, a group coaching program, and even hosted a virtual summit. Her message didn't just live on stage anymore—it lived in inboxes, downloads, and online communities. Now, instead of waiting for the next event to speak, she wakes up to Stripe notifications and emails from students around the world. Her brand became bigger than her schedule.

My Mindset Shift

For a long time, I believed speaking was *the thing.* The one big stage. The powerful keynote. The spotlight moment. But then I realized—the mic was just the beginning. Your message deserves more than 45 minutes on a stage. It deserves a platform. A movement. A body of work that lives on long after the applause. You can turn your story into a book. Your steps into a course. Your slides into a workshop. Your signature talk into a system. **You are the brand. The mic amplifies your voice—but your offers expand your impact.**

Common Mistakes and How to Avoid Them

- **Mistake:** Only relying on live speaking for income.
  Avoid it: Build products and programs that create impact long after the stage lights go out.
- **Mistake:** Trying to launch too many things at once.
  Avoid it: Start with one simple offer, test it, and grow from there.
- **Mistake:** Creating products without a clear audience.
  Avoid it: Build based on the needs and struggles of your ideal client, not just what sounds exciting.

Words of Wisdom

Your voice can move an audience, but your offers can change their lives long after the applause. Don't limit your influence to the stage — let your message live everywhere it can help someone grow.

Step-by-Step Action Plan: Expand Your Brand Beyond the Stage

1. Identify one core message from your keynote that can be developed into a product or program.
2. Choose one format to start with (course, coaching program, book, etc.).
3. Map out the steps or content needed for that offer. Use Canva for design.
4. Create a simple launch plan to share it with your audience.
5. Collect testimonials and feedback to refine and relaunch.

Quick Wins

- Write down three possible offers that extend your keynote.
- Poll your audience on what they'd love to learn from you next.
- Outline the first module of an online course.
- Create a lead magnet that leads into your new program.

Journal Prompt

If I could reach 10 times more people without speaking live, what would I create?

_____

_____

_____

Reflection

My biggest takeaway:

_____

My next move:

_____

Key Points to Remember

- Your keynote is a starting point, not the end.
- Products and programs create ongoing transformation.
- Digital offers give you scalability and freedom.
- Multiple streams of income make your business sustainable.

Mic Drop Moment

"Your stage is just the beginning — let your message travel the world."

Affirmation

"I expand my brand beyond the stage, creating offers that serve, inspire, and sustain my business."

Prompt for AI

Act as a product development coach. Create a plan to turn a 60-minute keynote into a 6-week online course with a companion workbook.

Smart Thinking: Take the stage, but don't stop there. Write the book. Launch the course. Start the podcast. Expand your influence and income without burning out.

Implementation Assignment- (there is a Canva demo on marshahudsonmedia.com)

Pick one product or program idea to expand your brand. Write a one-page outline of the format, who it serves, and the outcome it provides. Share it with one trusted colleague or potential client to get feedback before building it out.

Step Into the Spotlight Recap

Your brand doesn't stop at the stage—it multiplies when you expand it into products, programs, and digital offers. This is how you build sustainability, scalability, and legacy. Step into the spotlight by letting your message live far beyond the mic.

Speaker's Get Paid Checklist

- Choose one core message to expand into a product or program.
- Decide on your first new offer format.
- Outline your content or product structure.
- Create a launch plan to share it with your audience.
- Collect feedback to refine and improve.
- Add your new offer to your website and marketing materials.
- Promote it consistently through your talks, email list, and social media.
- Build in testimonials and case studies to increase credibility.
- Explore multiple formats over time (books, courses, memberships, etc.).
- Review your offers annually to ensure they align with your brand and audience needs.

Trainings for you as you grow or scale your coaching and speaking business

Podia https://marshalynnhudson.podia.com/

Youtube https://www.youtube.com/@MarshaLynnHudson

Payhip https://payhip.com/marshalynnhudson

Newsletter https://marshalynnhudson.substack.com/

Marsha Hudson Media https://marshahudsonmedia.com/

Chapter 15

Women Who Rock – Leave Your Legacy Now

"Your voice is more than a message — it's the legacy you leave behind."

You've done the work. You've built your message, refined your delivery, created offers, and expanded your brand. But there's one more step — stepping fully into the role of a woman who uses her voice, her influence, and her platform to create a lasting impact. This is where speaking becomes more than a business — it becomes your legacy.

Legacy isn't about waiting until you're "done" with your career or life. It's about being intentional with the impact you're making right now. The talks you give, the programs you launch, the clients you help — all of these moments are adding up to the story you'll leave behind. The truth is, the women who inspire generations aren't just known for their accomplishments — they're remembered for how they made people feel and the change they sparked.

You didn't come this far just to make noise. You came to make impact. To leave a legacy. To be remembered as the woman who showed up, spoke up, and helped others rise. Legacy isn't about perfection or fame. It's about planting seeds that grow into transformation long after you've left the room.

You leave your legacy when you say yes to the calling. Even when you're afraid. Even when you feel behind. Even when no one claps yet. You leave your legacy by showing up anyway, by sharing your story anyway, by standing on the stage even when your knees are shaking. This is what it means to rock the stage—and rock the world.

Your legacy is built one decision at a time. When you decide to turn your message into a movement. When you decide to turn your wisdom into a workshop. When you decide to stop shrinking and start sharing. Every choice adds to the ripple. Every conversation adds to the wave. And you never know who's watching or whose life will change because you were brave.

We live in a time where women's voices are needed more than ever. In boardrooms. In classrooms. On Zoom rooms. On stages. On podcasts. In books. Your voice carries history, healing, and hope. You don't need to go viral—you just need to be visible. When you show up with intention, your presence becomes power.

There's no perfect time to step out—just a right-now moment waiting for you to say yes. Don't wait until you have it all figured out. Don't wait for someone to hand you the mic. Pick it up. Use it. Speak from your scars, not just your strengths. Teach from what you've overcome. That's how people connect. That's how people transform.

As you grow, remember that legacy is about people, not platforms. It's not about how many likes, followers, or views you get. It's about who felt seen because of you. Who felt heard because of you. Who finally believed they could rise because you did it first. That's what they'll remember. That's what lives on.

You are already equipped with everything you need to leave a mark. Your life has prepared you. Your story has positioned you. Now your message will propel you. Don't minimize what you've built or downplay the journey. Own it. Walk in it. Teach it. Package it. And pass it on.

This book may end here—but your journey is just beginning. You are a Woman Who Rocks the Stage. Now go out there and shake the ground with your story, your voice, your power, and your purpose. The world is waiting.

Milestone Marker

By the end of this chapter, you should have:

- Defined what legacy means to you as a speaker and leader.
- Identified 1–2 ways you will intentionally share your message to impact future generations.
- Written a personal commitment statement about how you will continue to show up boldly.

Why Legacy Matters Now

We often think of legacy as something we leave later in life, but the truth is you are building it every single day. Every time you speak, mentor, or create something, you're planting seeds in someone else's future.

Here's the reality:

- Someone is making a decision because of your words.
- Someone is finding courage because you went first.
- Someone is dreaming bigger because you showed them it's possible.

When you own the fact that your work is shaping lives, you begin to show up with a new level of commitment, excellence, and purpose.

My Story: The Moment I Realized My Voice Was Bigger Than Me

I once received an email from a woman who had been in my audience months earlier. She told me that something I said — just one line in my talk — had stayed with her. She'd gone home, had a hard conversation with her boss, and negotiated a promotion she'd been scared to ask for. That one moment in my talk became a turning point in her career. It reminded me that what we say on stage can echo in someone's life for years — even when we don't know it.

The 3 L's of Leaving a Legacy

1. **Lead** – Be the example you want others to follow.
2. **Lift** – Use your platform to elevate other women's voices.
3. **Last** – Create work that continues to inspire, teach, and empower beyond your presence.

How to Build Your Legacy as a Speaker

Be Consistent: Keep showing up even when it's hard, even when the audience is small, even when it feels like no one is listening.
Be Generous: Share your knowledge freely in ways that serve beyond your paid work — podcasts, interviews, mentoring, community events.
Be Intentional: Say yes to opportunities that align with your mission and values, and don't be afraid to say no to the ones that don't.

Get Paid!

Leaving a legacy doesn't mean giving everything away for free — it means building impact and income together. The more you grow your influence, the more opportunities you create to be well-compensated for your expertise. Your legacy work — books, programs, speaking tours, collaborations — can continue to pay you and fund the causes you care about. Legacy is about sustainable impact, not burnout.

Think about it this way: your voice can be both your life's work and your life's wealth. When you combine purpose with profitability, you create something that lasts far beyond your own career.

Problem & Solution

Problem: Too many women play small, waiting for "someday" to make their mark.
Solution: Step fully into your influence now and make decisions that align with the legacy you want to leave.

Imagine this Scenario

She once questioned if her voice mattered. Now, her message is impacting women across generations. After refining her story and showing up boldly, she launched a podcast, published a book, and began mentoring other women.

What started as a desire to speak became a full movement.

She didn't wait for permission—she created her own platform, inspired hundreds, and became known as a woman who leads with purpose. Her ripple effect? Still growing.

My Mindset Shift

For years, I thought legacy was something you left behind. Now I know—legacy is something you live *right now*. It's not about being famous. It's about being faithful to the gift inside you. The message that only you can deliver. The story that someone else needs to hear so they can rise. You don't need to wait until you have the perfect website, a huge following, or a flawless pitch. You can show up boldly now—**with what you have, where you are, and who you are.** Every time you speak, post, teach, or lead— you're making impact. **Legacy isn't what you leave when you're done. It's what you build while you're walking in purpose.**

Common Mistakes and How to Avoid Them

- **Mistake:** Waiting until you "arrive" to think about legacy.
  Avoid it: Legacy isn't someday—it's built daily through consistency and impact.
- **Mistake:** Believing your story is too small to matter.
  Avoid it: Every story can spark change. Someone is waiting on your voice.
- **Mistake:** Keeping your message only tied to income.
  Avoid it: Legacy is about the ripple effect—the lives you touch, not just the checks you collect.

Words of Wisdom

Your voice is not just for this moment — it's for the generations coming after you. Every word you speak and every person you impact is part of your story. Make it count.

Step-by-Step Action Plan: Leave Your Legacy Now

1. Write down the three most important values you want to be known for.
2. Identify one way you can start living and leading by each of those values today.
3. Create a project or offer that aligns with your legacy vision.
4. Share your story more openly — someone needs to hear it now.
5. Choose one woman you can mentor or lift up this month.

Quick Wins

- Write your "legacy statement" in one sentence.
- Share one story from your journey on social media.
- Attend an event where you can connect with future collaborators.
- Send a thank-you note to someone who inspired your own journey.

Journal Prompt

If my speaking career ended today, what would I want to be remembered for?

_____

_____

_____

Reflection

My biggest takeaway:

_____

My next move:

_____

Key Points to Remember

- Your legacy starts now, not later.
- You influence more people than you realize.
- Leading, lifting, and lasting are the pillars of legacy.
- Align your work with your values to create impact that endures.

Mic Drop Moment

"The story you tell with your life will echo long after the stage lights fade."

Affirmation

"I am building a legacy of impact, influence, and inspiration every day I show up."

Prompt for AI

Act as a leadership coach. Create a 12-month plan for a speaker to grow her influence, income, and legacy through intentional action.

Smart Thinking: Your story, your voice, your courage—it all matters now. Don't wait until everything is perfect. Legacy begins the moment you decide to show up boldly, serve with purpose, and speak with heart.

Implementation Assignment

Write your **legacy statement.** Complete this sentence: "My voice will live on by...."

Then, identify one tangible step you can take this month to honor that legacy—whether it's writing a book, mentoring a younger speaker, or creating a program that lives on after you.

Step Into the Spotlight Recap

Your legacy isn't about perfection—it's about courage. Every time you show up, you give another woman permission to rise. Step into the spotlight by embracing your role as a legacy builder. The world doesn't just need your message today—it needs the ripple it will create for generations to come.

Speaker's Get Paid Checklist

- Define your legacy values and vision.
- Create offers and programs that reflect your mission.

- Share your story consistently across platforms.
- Mentor or collaborate with other women in your field.
- Choose partnerships that align with your values.
- Build assets (books, courses, memberships) that outlive the moment.
- Speak at events that align with your long-term goals.
- Document your journey to inspire others.
- Revisit your legacy plan annually
- Celebrate the lives you've touched along the way.

Trainings for you as you grow or scale your coaching and speaking business

Podia https://marshalynnhudson.podia.com/

Youtube https://www.youtube.com/@MarshaLynnHudson

Payhip https://payhip.com/marshalynnhudson

Newsletter https://marshalynnhudson.substack.com/

Marsha Hudson Media https://marshahudsonmedia.com/

https://www.facebook.com/groups/femaleentrepreneurswho buildbusinessesonline- facebook group

- For the free audio training to accompany this book- go to: https://marshalynnhudson.podia.com/

Conclusion

You've reached the end of this book, but this is not the end of your story. In fact, it's just the beginning. You've walked through the steps, the strategies, the mindset shifts, and the action plans. You've been equipped with tools and truths that can take your voice, your message, and your mission to the next level. Now, it's your turn to move.

You don't have to wait for permission, validation, or perfect timing. You've already got the wisdom, the story, and the calling. What's left is the decision to show up and do the work. There is someone out there waiting for your voice—waiting for your courage to unlock theirs. You may never meet them. But they will never forget you. That's legacy.

You don't need a massive platform to make massive impact. You don't need to be loud to be heard. You just need to be consistent. Authentic. Intentional. Real. Women who rock the stage don't pretend to have it all together— they show up with their full hearts and let people in. They speak truth. They speak life. And they create space for others to rise.

The path won't always be easy. Doubt will whisper. Fear will linger. But you are not the same woman who started reading this book. You are more aware. More ready. More aligned. The difference now is—you have a roadmap. You have a system. And you have a community of women who are rising with you.

So take the stage—whatever that looks like for you. Maybe it's a physical platform. Maybe it's a podcast. A Zoom room. A coaching group. A classroom. Wherever your feet are planted, that is your stage. Use it well. Own your story. Teach from your truth. Lead from your experience. Because your voice was never meant to be hidden. You are a Woman Who Rocks the Stage. Bold. Brilliant. Unstoppable. This world needs your voice, your story, and your leadership now more than ever. Keep rising. Keep speaking. And above all—keep walking in purpose with strength and grace. Your legacy is already in motion.

Mic Drop Moment: Own the Stage, Leave the Legacy

You didn't come this far just to inspire people—you came to **transform** them. You didn't write your story just to be heard—you wrote it so others could heal. You didn't choose this path for applause—you chose it for **impact**. And now, you stand at the edge of something extraordinary. You have the voice, the vision, and the victory story. Not because everything has been easy—but because you rose anyway. Again and again. Speak with fire. Lead with heart. Teach with power. Your story is your strategy. Your pain became your platform. Your life is the proof—and that's what makes you unstoppable.

This is your moment. This is your mic drop. Now go rock the stage—because the world is waiting for YOU.

More Resources You Want to Spend Time Checking Out

- **The 8-Bundle Resource Pack** – Eight free PDF guides designed to help you build momentum and stay consistent. (https://payhip.com/marshalynnhudson)
- **Mini Courses & Trainings** – Short, actionable trainings to help you master your message, build your brand, and create income streams. (https://marshalynnhudson.podia.com/)
- **Scripts & Templates** – Plug-and-play resources so you never get stuck on what to say or how to structure your talks, calls, or proposals. (resources section)
- **Proposals & Pitch Materials** – Professional examples to help you land speaking engagements and paid opportunities with confidence. (links in the resources section)
- **My YouTube Channel** – Weekly videos where I share strategies, stories, and systems to keep you growing. (https://www.youtube.com/@MarshaLynnHudson)
- **Substack Newsletter** – Exclusive content, behind-the-scenes insights, and encouragement delivered straight to your inbox

Trainings for you as you grow or scale your coaching and speaking business

Podia https://marshalynnhudson.podia.com/

Payhip https://payhip.com/marshalynnhudson

Marsha Hudson Media https://marshahudsonmedia.com/

https://www.facebook.com/groups/femaleentrepreneurswho buildbusinessesonline (facebook group)

Bonus: How to Rock the Stage Anywhere You Show Up

You don't always control where you're asked to speak. Sometimes it's a webinar, sometimes a boardroom, sometimes a large stage. But you can control how you show up. This bonus section will give you practical strategies to shine no matter where your audience is.

Section 1: Rocking the Virtual Stage

The virtual stage is here to stay. Whether it's Zoom, a webinar, or a social media live stream, virtual speaking requires energy, intentionality, and tech confidence.

Tips to Rock the Virtual Stage

- Set the Stage: Lighting should be in front of you (not behind). Use a neutral background or branded banner. Clear audio is even more important than video.
- Eye Contact: Look into the camera lens, not at the screen. It creates the feeling of intimacy, like you're speaking directly to each person.
- Energy Amplified: Online, your energy must be 15–20 percent higher than in person. Smile more, use hand gestures, and vary your voice tone to keep attention.
- Engagement is Everything: Keep attention by asking questions, using the chat, or adding polls. Build in interaction every 5–7 minutes.
- Be Concise: Break content into short segments. Use slides sparingly, and highlight one key point at a time.

- Have a Clear CTA: Share a freebie, drop a link in the chat, or flash a QR code at the end.

Example: Imagine running a 30-minute webinar. You could start with a question in the chat ("What's your biggest speaking struggle?"), teach three confidence tips, run a quick poll halfway through, and close with a free toolkit download.

Action Step: Record yourself teaching one tip for five minutes on Zoom. Watch the replay and check your lighting, energy, and eye contact. Adjust and repeat until you look engaging and confident.

Section 2: Rocking the Face-to-Face Stage

When you're live and in-person, presence is everything. The way you walk on stage, your body language, and your ability to connect physically with the room determine how memorable you are.

Tips to Rock the Face-to-Face Stage

- Own Your Entrance: Step on stage confidently, pause, smile, and let the audience settle before you speak. It shows authority.
- Move with Purpose: Walk the stage or the room intentionally. Don't pace nervously—move toward different sections of the audience to draw them in.
- Command Body Language: Stand tall, keep your shoulders back, and use open gestures. Make eye contact with individuals in different parts of the room.
- Involve the Audience: Ask for a show of hands, invite quick reflections, or let them share with a partner for 30 seconds.

- Use Vocal Variety: Adjust your pace, volume, and tone to keep interest. Pauses are powerful—use them after key points.
- Close Strong: End with a short story, a memorable phrase, or a clear invitation.

Example: At a women's conference, instead of only lecturing, you might say: "Turn to the woman next to you and share one fear you want to leave behind today." That moment creates connection and energy in the room.

Action Step: The next time you're in a room (even if you're not speaking), practice "owning the space." Walk slowly, stand tall, and make eye contact with three people. Notice how different the room feels when you intentionally take up space with confidence.

Section 3: Captivating Any Audience, Anywhere

Whether you're on a podcast, leading a small workshop, presenting at work, or even giving a toast, the art of captivating an audience is universal.

Tips to Captivate Anywhere

- Lead with a Hook: Start with a question, a bold statement, or a story. The first 30 seconds set the tone.
- Focus on Transformation: Always ask yourself, "What do I want them to think, feel, or do after this?" Shape your message around that outcome.
- Clarity is Queen: Use simple words, short sentences, and strong pauses. Complicated language loses attention.

- Read the Room: Pay attention to energy. A boardroom may need calm authority, while a women's retreat may invite warmth and passion.
- Consistency of Story and Invitation: Have one signature story and one signature invitation you can use in almost any setting. This keeps you confident and prepared.
- Adapt Quickly: If tech fails, if your slides won't load, or if your time gets cut, smile, simplify, and keep going. Audiences admire a speaker who handles challenges with grace.

Example: On a podcast, instead of rambling, you might start with: "I used to think only big stages mattered, but my first client came from a 15-minute webinar. Here's why…" That short hook keeps listeners tuned in.

Action Step: Write down one signature story and one signature invitation you can use anywhere. Practice delivering both in two minutes. That way, whether you're on Zoom, in a meeting, or on stage, you'll always be ready.

Closing Thought

The true power of a woman who rocks the stage isn't just in the size of the platform—it's in her ability to adapt her presence and captivate hearts anywhere.

Whether online, face-to-face, or in between, your job is to:

- Connect with authenticity.
- Serve with generosity.
- Invite with confidence.

That's how you captivate and impact any audience, anywhere you show up.

- For the free audio training to accompany this book - go to: https://marshalynnhudson.podia.com/

Resources to Help You Rock the Stage

I don't want you to just read this book—I want you to have the tools, templates, and training you need to put it into action. That's why I've created a resource hub packed with everything you need to grow your speaking and coaching business.

Inside, you'll find:

- **The 8-Bundle Resource Pack** – Eight free PDF guides designed to help you build momentum and stay consistent.
- **Mini Courses & Trainings** – Short, actionable trainings to help you master your message, build your brand, and create income streams.
- **Scripts & Templates** – Plug-and-play resources so you never get stuck on what to say or how to structure your talks, calls, or proposals.
- **Proposals & Pitch Materials** – Professional examples to help you land speaking engagements and paid opportunities with confidence.
- **My YouTube Channel** – Weekly videos where I share strategies, stories, and systems to keep you growing.
- **Substack Newsletter** – Exclusive content, behind-the-scenes insights, and encouragement delivered straight to your inbox.
- This page is your go-to library—curated to help you keep moving forward long after you've turned the last page of this book. Bookmark it, revisit it, and use these tools as you continue your journey to becoming a woman who rocks the stage.

- **Trainings for you as you grow or scale your coaching and speaking business**

- Podia https://marshalynnhudson.podia.com/

- Youtube https://www.youtube.com/@MarshaLynnHudson

- Payhip https://payhip.com/marshalynnhudson

- Newsletter https://marshalynnhudson.substack.com/

- Marsha Hudson Media https://marshahudsonmedia.com/

- https://www.facebook.com/groups/femaleentrepren eurswhobuildbusinessesonline (facebook group)

Special Speaker Resource Bundle- (Go to https://payhip.com/b/k4aW0)

Signature Talk Outline Template

Step-by-step structure for creating a powerful, engaging, and client-converting talk.

2. Discovery Call Script

A full script to confidently lead calls, ask the right questions, handle objections, and close with ease.

3. Pitch Email Template

Customizable email with subject line ideas, body copy, and follow-up language for pitching yourself to events, podcasts, or organizations.

4. Speaker One-Sheet Sample

What to include on a one-sheet: bio, headshot, signature talks, audience takeaways, testimonials, and contact info.

5. Speaker Toolkit Checklist

Comprehensive checklist of essentials every speaker needs (bio, media kit, talk outline, reel, testimonials, etc.).

6. Sample Speaker Proposal

A professional proposal template with sections for overview, session description, objectives, engagement style, deliverables, investment, and next steps.

7. 30 Storytelling Social Media Post Starters

Thirty prompts to help you share authentic stories that connect with your audience and build your brand.

8. LinkedIn DM Script

A simple, non-salesy script to start conversations with potential clients, collaborators, or event organizers.

9. Tool Recommendations

Curated list of recommended tools (Canva, Podia, Payhip, Zoom, Trello, Kit, Hello Audio and Calendly) to simplify your speaking and coaching business.

www.marshalynnhudson.com

www.marshahudsonmedia.com

To your abundant success,

Marsha Lynn Hudson- The Queen of Systems

www.ingramcontent.com/pod-product-compliance
Lightning Source LLC
Chambersburg PA
CBHW051307120626
46547CB00015B/2129